CORTINA

629.222
ROB

34715866 2

SOUTH
YRSH
BRARIES

CONTENTS

CORTINA

INTRODUCTION & ACKNOWLEDGEMENTS

Introduction

In 1962 the new Ford Cortina changed the face of the British motor industry, and it made a big impression on me at the time. Those were the days when I was a small-car enthusiast, but I soon saw that the Cortina was going to change everything – and I bought one. The first of a new breed of Ford motor cars, it was also the original of many clones from rival British marques.

Although its introduction was a gamble, for Ford that gamble soon paid off. From 1963 and for most of the next two decades the Cortina was the UK market leader, not only selling faster than any previous Ford but selling faster than any other British car of its day.

By the time Ford built the last car in 1982, the Cortina had re-invented the British automotive market. More than four million Cortinas had been built and sold, the cars had re-defined the company car market sector, and a number of reputations had blossomed with their success.

Even before it was finally dropped from production, the Cortina had become an icon. Television programmes had been made about it, London's Victoria and Albert Museum had organised an exhibition around it, and most of Ford's rivals had developed new models to compete with it.

No-one could have foreseen this in the early 1960s. When the car was announced, Britain was wallowing in Mini-mania, and anything that did not match up to Alec Issigonis's front-wheel-drive creation was spurned. Predictably, the Cortina was widely derided by the current motoring media at first, and it took years of success – in the market-place and in motorsport – for the respect to follow.

By the end of 1960s, the Cortina's reputation was secure for all time. New cars were flooding out of Dagenham, used examples were seen on virtually every high street and front driveway in the country, and Ford was always happy to develop new types to keep up the momentum. For more than another decade there were few problems in selling up to 200,000 cars a year.

By the time the Cortina retired, its life and times were an object lesson for all other car companies on how to research, develop and, most importantly, market such a product successfully. Inevitably, one day that story would have to be told.

When I took on the job I looked for a new angle. Here, I decided, was a car for which product planning was always more important that mechanical design and marketing had always outranked innovation. Accordingly, I spent much time talking to the important personalities who had influence on the marketing side, rather than to the engineers who had followed their bidding.

This explains why lengthy comments from Sir Terence Beckett and Sam Toy (both of whom went on to become chairmen of Ford-UK), from Hamish Orr-Ewing, who was in at the very start of the Cortina product, and from Walter Hayes, who did so much to establish the image in the market-place, are so prominent. Harry Calton, whose distinguished Ford career spanned the entire life of the Cortina, also exercised his total memory recall to fill in the gaps.

Looking back, I suppose it was inevitable that, being an author, I would write a book about Ford Cortinas one day, for in the 1960s my life seemed to be filled with them. I owned several and rallied in many others; I road tested fleets of them, wrote about dozens more and sampled scores over the years. I might not have known as much about the project as Ford managers always did, but I always seemed to be close to the latest models.

After running a Consul Mk I for a decade, my father bought his first Cortina Mk I 1200 in 1963, and I bought the first of two Cortina Mk I 1500GTs in 1965. Between 1963 and 1965 I must have started more than fifty British rallies as a co-driver in Mk I GTs, and there was one unforgettable occasion when I co-drove Roger Clark's Lotus-Cortina to an international rally victory.

At this time, Cortinas seemed to be involved in so much of my life. I used them for business and for pleasure. There were the nights when I used my own GTs to report on rallies and slept in them. There were the 'works' rally cars I borrowed, road tested, parked in my drive (and flaunted to all the neighbours). There were the race cars I used to see on the tracks of the UK and write about with such glee. There was the Mk IV 2300S in which a colleague of mine was once clocked for speeding at a most unlikely rate in rural Dorset (and I was an oh-so-innocent passenger). There was the Mk V with a damaged gearbox at the press launch in Devon – my fault entirely. There was ... no, that's quite enough nostalgia for one page.

Except for the Lotus-Cortinas of the 1960s, Cortinas were mechanically simple cars and so nothing like the equivalent of Mini-mania ever developed around them. They were, on the other hand, amazingly popular for a very long time, so their story needs to be told.

It has, of course, been quite impossible to cram every detail of the Cortina's twenty-year career into one book; I hope that the highlights, at least, are all here.

Acknowledgements

First and foremost, I want to thank the five major Ford personalities who helped me put this story together in 1997:

Hamish Orr-Ewing: Ford analyst, product planner and later the Chairman of Jaguar and of Rank Zerox.

Sir Terence Beckett: 'Mr Cortina' to Fleet Street who started his Ford management life in Sir Patrick Hennessy's office and ended it as Ford's Chairman.

Sam Toy: extrovert and archetypal salesman who pushed the Cortina to its greatest heights before becoming Chairman of Ford in 1980.

Walter Hayes: ex-Fleet Street editor who moved to Ford in 1961, completely modernising the company's image in the 1960s and 1970s. Later he became Chairman of Aston Martin, and revitalised that company too. He was the guru other authors like to consult when the soul, philosophy and great achievements of the company are concerned.

Harry Calton: 'office boy' in the press office in 1952 who rose rapidly through the ranks of the Public Affairs Department, was always close to Walter Hayes and was ever present when new Cortinas made their appearance. In later life he took over as Director of Public Affairs at Aston Martin Lagonda Ltd.

Then, of course, there are other Ford people who have helped me so often and so patiently over the years:

Stuart Turner: ruthlessly successful Director of Motorsport in the 1970s and the 1980s with several years at the helm of Public Affairs; a man with a wonderful memory to tap when the going gets tough.

Rod Mansfield: one of the few 'characters' Ford allowed to emerge from Engineering. As head of the Special Vehicle Engineering Department, he knew more than most about Ford cars and their components.

Derek Sansom: public relations expert and adviser to Ford. He gently educated me about the way Ford keeps in touch with Cortina enthusiasts and with the one-make clubs.

Although everyone at Ford has always helped me to indulge my nostalgic streak, without the Photographic Department I could never have illustrated this book in such variety. Over the years, managers from Steve Clark to Barry Reynolds and Steve Woolmington let me trawl through the extensive archive while the ladies who administer it – Sheila Knapman and Fran Chamberlain – put up with me for day after day.

I'm eternally grateful to all of them for letting me sift through the massive and impressive record of Ford's past and for taking the time to explain where everything was stored and what it all meant.

I'm very lucky – and grateful – to have been allowed to consult Ford's archive, for almost all the illustrations in this book come from that source. Sheila Knapman and Fran Chamberlain always gave me the impression that they considered no request too bizarre.

I also want to give a heartfelt and general thank you to all the one-make clubs who have ensured the Cortina's continuing survival. My particular thanks to Steve Kerr, Malcolm Rugman and Jane Rugman of the Mk I Owners' Club who helped me with facts, figures and pictures.

Graham Robson
Burton Bradstock, England

1

THE 'ARCHBISHOP' PROJECT

When the original Cortina was launched in 1962, critics formed a line to say that Ford had got it all wrong; by 1982 – when more than four million cars had been built – they had all eaten their words. By any standards, the Cortina project had been a huge success.

Much of the early criticism – from the media and indeed from Ford dealers – stemmed from the car's simplicity. In an era when the complex, new front-wheel-drive Mini was making all the headlines, the media was thirsting for more of the same. Perhaps they didn't understand the implications – especially the economic ones – but they knew what they liked.

You know the sort of thing. In Britain, Minis had transversely mounted engines and rubber suspensions, while in Europe, the latest Renaults were rear-engined, with four-wheel disc brakes. In North America, GM was building Corvairs with rear-mounted flat-six air-cooled engines. Faced with that, the media reasoned, surely Ford's conventional, 'old-fashioned' Cortina was a big mistake?

Ford and its managers listened politely to all the criticism, smiled sweetly, and took no offence. Within months, the sales figures proved their point. The Cortina was what the public – particularly the business public – wanted, and it soon became a best-seller, dominating British sales charts for the next twenty years. Ford never

Sir Patrick Hennessy (1898-1981)

Pat Hennessy was born in Southern Ireland. In 1920 he joined the Henry Ford & Son tractor-making factory in Cork, where he soon made a name for himself in management, and moved on to Dagenham in 1931, when the new factory opened for business.

Rising rapidly through the Purchase Department, he took over as Ford-UK's General Manager in 1939, and ran the company until 1968. He was knighted in 1941 for his work during World War 2 (when Ford factories produced an astonishing number of Rolls-Royce Merlin aero-engines and cross-country Bren-gun carriers). In 1948 he took over as Managing Director, moving upwards to become Chairman in 1956.

Although he had been ready to retire in 1963 – the year after the Cortina was launched – Henry Ford II persuaded him to stay on as Chairman, though Managing Director Allen Barke then became Ford-UK's Chief Executive.

Sir Patrick finally retired in 1968, which means that he had been at the top of Ford-UK for twenty years of excitement and expansion. Even then he retained an office at Ford's Grafton Street premises in central London.

He seemed to know everyone in public and private life, numbering figures such as Lord Beaverbrook among his friends (which always helped his – and Ford's – projects immeasurably). By any standards he was a formidable businessman, and there is no doubt that he was one of the most shrewd, yet dynamic, industrialists the UK has ever seen.

Although the Cortina would be no larger or more powerful than the original 1950 Consul had been, it would be much lighter, better looking and more fuel efficient – all with a 1.2-litre engine.

had to make any excuses for the car – except for apologising when waiting lists grew too long.

First thoughts

In spite of what publicists would have you believe, there is no such thing as a new car which leaps, fully formed, from its creator's mind on day one. Although detailed work on the Cortina began in 1960, its influences stretched back much further than that.

Ford of Britain had built its first car – the American-designed Model T – in 1911, and the company soon became a major player in the British motor industry, with the Model T as market leader. The company opened its new Dagenham factory in 1931, and the very first small Ford – the 8hp Model Y – followed in 1932, after which the company was invariably third in the British sales chart (behind Austin and Morris).

After World War 2, a period in which Ford had built thousands of Rolls-Royce Merlin aero engines

and mountains of other military equipment, the company settled down to rather turbulent peacetime conditions. Faced with a seemingly limitless demand for cars in the UK, but with government exhortations to 'export or die,' the company could always sell more cars than it could make.

Sir Patrick Hennessy, the Irish-born manager who had originally joined Ford in 1920, became Managing Director in 1948, and for the next two decades ran Ford of Britain with very little interference from Detroit. Henry Ford II, in fact, trusted him so much that he rarely questioned anything proposed by Sir Patrick.

Walter Hayes, Ford's dynamic Public Affairs chief when the Cortina made its mark, thinks he knows why:

'If ever there was a man of the world, it was Hennessy – he had, after all, been Lord Beaverbrook's number one man during the war. He was a friend of Churchill's, he was

Terry Beckett, an economist by training and an engineering enthusiast, joined Ford in 1950. From the mid-1950s he ran Ford's Product Planning Department and, with Hamish Orr-Ewing, was responsible to a great extent for the skeleton of the 'Archbishop' project. Later he became Ford's Chairman and Managing Director, and received a knighthood.

a member of The Other Club – so he knew everybody. He was a highly sophisticated and intelligent man.

'He had been a marvellous rugby player, he went to the very best tailor in Saville Row, he had the most marvellous knowledge and dry wit ...'

By the 1950s, in fact, Ford of Britain was not merely being managed by Hennessy, but was increasingly fashioned in his image. Everything it was and everything it did came about because of his decisions, and he was not all worried by jibes that British Fords were 'Dagenham Dustbins,' for this was just one wounding nickname promoted by Ford's opposition, or by the rather backwoods attitudes of some of his dealers.

At this time, Ford's range of cars had settled down into three distinct families. In modern language, the

'entry level' model was the Popular, a 1930s-style Anglia of obsolete design, which had been further cheapened; there were mass-market Anglia 100Es and Prefects with side-valve engines and three-speed transmissions, and a range of much larger Consuls, Zephyrs and Zodiacs.

In the meantime, Hennessy had set up the so-called Product Staff department (which later took on the more understandable title of Product Planning). This was originally run by Martin Tustin, who was then head-hunted by Standard-Triumph. The job was consequently taken over by Terry Beckett after nine months.

Nowadays, as all authors know, Ford is reluctant to build up its 'personalities,' but for the next decade Terry Beckett was certainly an exception. By the time the new Cortina was ready for launch, he had become 'Mr Cortina' – inside the company and to the world outside.

All was not, however, sweetness and light, for Beckett's department was soon hated (and sometimes resisted) within the company, both

The Anglia 105E, which appeared in 1959, was the first Ford to use the completely new oversquare four-cylinder engine that would also be pivotal to the Cortina. Although this Anglia would become Ford's first million-seller, the Cortina would get there much faster.

The Classic 109E appeared in 1961, really a larger statement of the Anglia 105E. Complete with 1.34-litre engine and reverse-slope rear window, it was too heavy for its class and would have a short life.

by the Sales and Manufacturing staffs – so he was grateful for Hennessy's continued support, and for that of the all-powerful Finance department:

'We were building a new framework, organisationally, and in terms of people as well. It was a change of culture, and I have to tell you that by the time we came to plan the Cortina, the difficulty was that we had been through two models that had really got badly out of control.'

Those two cars, incidentally, were the Consul/Zephyr Mk II, and the Anglia 105E/Classic 109E programmes. To the outside world, they were great successes but, to Beckett, there had been major shortcomings:

'We had to get control of our costs. We weren't going to try to control the cost of everything in the car, we were going to control the cost of what we called the "key parts." If we could control those, we were already in control of about 90 per cent of the car.

'We also triangulated the cost of these from existing Ford parts which were similar, and with the best of competitive practice. I had endless examinations of all our competitors' costs; we examined every detail, to see if we could learn anything from them in terms of manufacturing processes, design,

customer benefits, and so on. We were able to triangulate the key parts – there were about 500 of these – and we put them in what we called a Red Book.'

One of Beckett's more junior colleagues, Hamish Orr-Ewing, came to specialise in what Ford-speak called 'Light Car Product Planning,' and in the next few years it was Orr-Ewing, taking advice from Engineering, Manufacturing, Sales and, of course, Finance, who developed all the details of the Cortina's layout, with Terry Beckett as his manager.

Orr-Ewing, unlike Beckett, was a car-nut, through and through. With a father who had once owned a Rolls-Royce Silver Ghost, and a period working in the RAC Competitions Department, this almost went without saying. Having joined Ford in the advertising department, he soon moved to Product Planning, where his first task was to monitor the new Anglia 105E's progress towards the assembly line: 'Perhaps the one significant benchmark that I can claim is that I persuaded Terry and, in due course, Engineering to put a 1200 option into the Anglia – it had definitely not been thought of in the first phase. There was quite a lot of resistance to that, in fact ...'

Gradually, in the late 1950s, Sir Patrick Hennessy, Terry Beckett,

Orr-Ewing and many others began to look ahead for what they originally called 'a new Prefect.' It was to be a new model which would fill a gap between the Anglia 105E and the existing Consul Mk II – in size, performance and price.

It was not, incidentally, intended to take the place of that strange offshoot the 109E Classic – famous for its reverse-slope rear window style – and the rather transatlantic Capri coupé developed from it which came on the scene in 1961.

Orr-Ewing describes the Classic as a 'complete red herring,' and although Terry Beckett admits that he was, of course, responsible for its planning, he is also somewhat dismissive:

'The Classic should have been launched soon after the Anglia 105E, but because of an engine shortage it was delayed for about nine months. It was heavy but it was a good solid motor car in every way. I think that, had we been prepared to go on in a humdrum kind of way, then the Classic would always have been acceptable.'

By 1960, therefore, Product Planning thought they knew what a 'new Prefect' had to include, and what should be avoided at all costs. In simple terms, the company wanted to be able to provide incredible value for money – they wanted to produce a medium-sized car for a small-car price. If not impossible, this was going to be extremely difficult. The new car would need to be larger

The Classic 109E of 1961 had the reverse-slope rear window style first seen in the UK on the Anglia 105E of 1959. Although the Cortina would be almost the same size as the Classic, it was a much lighter, more practical and more successful car in every way.

than the existing Anglia, but much lighter than the Classic, and – most important, this – it needed to be more profitable than any previous Ford model.

'Cardinal' and Mini – major influences

As is now clear, two other new car projects affected the 'new Prefect' considerably – one being the Ford-USA / Ford-Germany 'Cardinal' model and the other BMC's new Mini:

'We had to face the fact at Ford,' Terry Beckett recalls, 'that the Mini had arrived, and outflanked us on the price scale. We also knew that BMC was going to introduce a bigger version of the Mini, the 1100, and that this would get over the defects of the Mini – this was a much more impressive offering than the Mini, what would it do to us ?'

Then there was the Cardinal:

'Ford of Germany were very concerned about their 12M, and they desperately needed a replacement for it – they needed something really imaginative. It was then decided that what Germany needed would also be absolutely splendid for the USA – they would have a front-wheel-drive car ... and they would make this available not only for Germany but also for the United States.'

The idea was that the Cardinal would be built from body shells made in Germany and in the United States; front-wheel-drive transaxles would be produced in Germany (which was at that time a cheaper place to make things) and shipped to the USA. As we now know (see the panel on page 18) this grand strategy collapsed when Ford-USA cancelled their end of the deal, though Cardinal became the Taunus 12M and Taunus 15M in time to compete on all fronts with the Cortina.

At first sight, the Mini – with its predatory pricing – terrified Ford, for they could see no way of getting their Anglia costs down to the same level. So, how had BMC done it? Terry Beckett knew he would have to move fast:

'As soon as the Mini came out in 1959, I waylaid one on the way to a dealer. Without taking it to pieces, I went right over it, spent a couple of hours on it, and I could see straight away that it was of such complexity, it had so much in it, that there was no way that they [BMC] could be producing it for there to be any profit at that price.

'Two weeks later, we then bought one, and stripped it right down, and because we were dissatisfied, we did it all again, right down to the spot welds. We examined every part of it – and there wasn't any way that they could be making money.'

The saga of how Ford then alerted BMC's Managing Director, Sir George Harriman, telling him that BMC was likely to go bust unless it raised prices, and that Ford would follow if it tried to match them, is well-documented – and is a sad reflection on BMC's methods. Harriman was arrogant enough to insist that he was a production engineer by training, and knew what he was doing ...

In the long run, of course, BMC did indeed go bust (which brought about the merger with Leyland ...) and Ford was stubborn enough to persist with its own sound pricing policies.

The Cardinal, and its implications on Ford-UK's export prospects, was a more serious problem. In several European countries, Ford-UK and Ford-Germany competed head-on, their cars actually displayed, side-by-side in the same showrooms.

This was all part of what was vividly known at Ford as the 'two-fishing-line' approach – the theory being that *overall* sales would always increase. The problem as far as Ford-UK was concerned was that unless they could find something to bait a vacant hook, then from 1962-63 the Cardinal would have no in-house competition.

Sir Patrick Hennessy, who was not consulted about the Cardinal, nor invited to take any part in the development of the transatlantic programme, was furious. Hamish Orr-Ewing thinks he knows why:

'I assume that Hennessy was regarded as too dominant a figure for a complete co-operation between the USA and an overseas subsidiary. This annoyed Hennessy, and what in effect created the Cortina was that he told Terry Beckett in absolutely unambiguous terms that we, Ford-UK, using developments of our existing drive lines, would produce a new vehicle which would, in every way, outperform, under-cost, and would be available as early, as the Cardinal.

There was a high level of emotion in Pat Hennessy's decision. That is not to say it was wise – it was brilliant.'

Within days – hours, some reckon – all thought of developing a 'new Prefect' had taken a back seat, replaced by the simple, strategic, nationalistic aim of beating the Germans.

The new car needed a project name, if only so that everyone at Ford could know what they were talking about at planning meetings. Several people at Ford are linked with the invention of this name, because it became legendary, but Hamish Orr-Ewing's version is probably authentic:

'The Americans had called their car "Cardinal," after the bird, which we knew perfectly well, but because they hadn't been very helpful, and because it pleased my sense of humour, I said: "Why don't we call ours 'Archbishop'..."

On the basis that it would outrank a Cardinal ?

'More or less, yes! Quite honestly, this was to tweak their tails a bit. I told Terry, who thought it would be a good idea, and promised to have a word with Sir Patrick ...' Which is what happened. Hennessy took the name on board, and promptly forgot about its origins, except that:

'At a very late stage, a name for the market place was being discussed,' Orr-Ewing recalls. 'Archie Barnes was a senior production man in Dagenham, occasionally called in to the Product Committee. The question of a name went on for hours and hours – until Archie actually suggested that the car be called "Archbishop" in public!

'To which there was a slight titter, and aghast expressions. I can remember Sir Patrick looking at him for a time, and very quietly saying: "Thank you Archie." Nothing more was said ...'

All this came to a head in the spring of 1960 when Sir Patrick told Terry Beckett and Fred Hart (Executive Engineer, Light Cars) that he was determined to match the Cardinal – and immediately there was a timing crisis. Work on the Cardinal/Taunus 12M had already been going ahead for a year, but since Sir Patrick was determined to launch his new car at the same time, this gave his team less than two years to turn a good idea into cars rolling down the assembly tracks at Dagenham:

'And we did it,' Sir Terence reminded me. 'The Cortina came in under cost *and* in terms of investment costs, and most significantly of all, we did it in record time. I believe we took just 21 months from full-size clay style to Job 1 [in Ford-speak, this means when the very first production-standard car was completed], which was an all-time record for the industry, and certainly for Ford.'

Shaping the Cortina

Even before the stylists, led by American-born Roy Brown, began their work, Beckett and Orr-Ewing took advice from all sides, added in their own experience and presented a detailed brief to Sir Patrick Hennessy for approval. By this time, incidentally, Hamish Orr-Ewing had gained a young administrative assistant, Alex Trotman. Thirty years later, of course, Trotman became Ford's top man – top, that is, of the parent company and every other subsidiary:

'He was the single biggest contributor to my programme. There was also another man,' Hamish told me, 'called Peter Fearn. He went off his head later on, and became a hippy in South America.

At that time, there is no doubt that Ford was terrified by the promise of the still-secret BMC 1100, which their espionage had shown to be quite roomy, very attractively styled and with a much better ride than the Mini. Terry Beckett explained why:

'We were desperately concerned about the 1100. We decided that we needed a bigger body shell, and we also needed more wheel movement. We needed more width in the body – there was no question of using pedals offset to the steering column. We also decided that we would provide a proper boot – and in the end it was a very generous boot. In a way we overdid it a bit, but it was perfect for a rep who wanted to take samples around with him; it was perfect for the family man who wanted to pack the wife, kids, luggage and all that – the Mini didn't cope with this, nor did the 1100.'

The most basic decision, however, was to forget all about front-wheel-drive and go for developed versions of the Anglia 105E engine, gearbox and axle. Walter Hayes, who had recently arrived as Hennessy's Public Affairs guru, knows why:

'It was obvious that front-wheel-drive was becoming glamorous, and there was an element of "why wasn't Ford of Britain doing front-wheel-drive?"...

'In the first place, though, we had to spend £19 million in launching the Cortina, and Hennessy knew perfectly well that if he was going to invest a lot of money to re-tool factories, particularly to make transaxles,

he would have ended up with a car that would really not have met his cost objectives ...

'We actually had a little front-wheel-drive prototype which we'd built, and Hennessy had done all the costings on this prototype, so he knew what he was talking about. In any event, I think Hennessy always had a somewhat better feeling about the car as a functional instrument in people's hands, rather than as a technological marvel. Also, of course, he was very aware of the market place ...'

Terry Beckett confirms this:

'One thing that Pat Hennessy really claims the credit for was the establishment up at Lodge Road in Birmingham which was called Advance Engineering. The reason for it being up there was that we could more easily get engineers in the Midlands who wouldn't come down to settle in Essex!

'They had been working for two years on front-wheel-drive cars. The state of the art at that time was that we discovered that we could not solve that final transmission problem – it sounds incredible today, but that was the state of the art.

'One of Pat Hennessy's great talents was that, in spite of being quite a flamboyant entrepreneur, a piratical figure in many ways, he had a very keen sense of the limitations of any situation, so he said: "We are not ready for front-wheel-drive."'

For all these, and other

compelling economic reasons, Ford therefore elected to design a conventional car – not conventional in terms of value for money, or size-to-weight ratio, but conventional in layout, with a classic type of Ford drive-line. Working under the American-born engineering chief Victor Raviolo, Fred Hart's team spent months scheming the layout of a medium-sized saloon, which formed the basis of the styling work.

Dimensionally, the two basic decisions were to develop the 'Archbishop' project around a 98-inch wheelbase and an overall length of 168 inches. This is how the new car compared with existing (and planned) Fords:

Although the 'Archbishop' appeared to be a car of similar size to the Classic 109E, Ford has always shrugged off any connection between the two. (This car, incidentally, would not be announced until 1961, by which time the Cortina was already being developed.) The Classic 109E, not to put too fine a point on it, used a structure with the same type of 'cut-and-carve' engineering as the Anglia 105E. According to Harry Calton, who would soon become intimately connected with the launch of the Cortina:

'The engineers always said that the Classic was the last Ford we ever built to the "Safari spec." – one of those models that we took out to East Africa and did all the

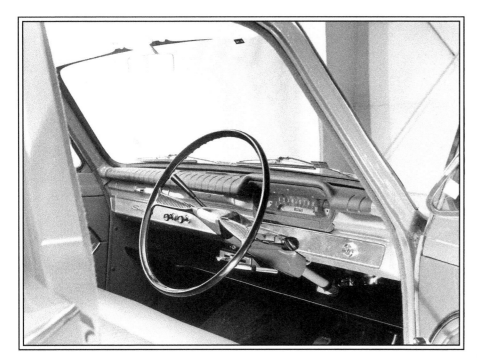

Left and below: The first-generation 'Archbishop' models, soon to be named Cortina, had a very simple fascia layout, some fitted with a steering-column gearchange, some with a centre floor change.

development there. The Classic was grossly overweight, and that three-bearing engine – the 1340cc unit – really wasn't the marvel of the age ...

'Yet people who bought Classics seemed to be happy with them, but it was rather unfortunately styled, with that enormous boot ...'

Grossly overweight? Judge for yourselves. The original two-door Classic weighed 2025lb, whereas the first two-door Cortinas weighed only 1725lb. For the Cortina, therefore, new techniques resulted in a saving of 300lb – the weight, say, of the average husband-and-wife partnership.

Styling work began in the spring of 1960, the brief being that this car would be built in two-door saloon, four-door saloon and five-door estate car forms. Feasibility engineers (who worked hand-in-hand with the stylists to make sure that what was proposed could actually be built, economically and in huge quantities) also had to note that Ford planned to export complete kits for final assembly in countries as close as Southern Ireland, and as remote as Australia.

A great deal of development was needed before a clay-model style (of the two-door saloon) was signed off in November 1960, with the four-door following it in April 1961, and the estate car in September. Although the overall size never changed significantly in that time,

Model	Wheelbase (inches)	Overall length (in.)
Anglia 105E	90.5	153.5
Archbishop/Cortina	98	168
Classic 109E	99	170.7
Consul Mk 2	104.5	173

Although the Cortina was no larger than the Classic which it soon displaced, there was more space in the rear. This was a 1963 model with the two-door body style.

Below: Every Cortina Mk I saloon was famous for those circular tail lamps, and the vee-profile junction of the boot lid and the rear cross-panel.

there seemed to be endless versions of the side and the tail.

American influence was everywhere – not only because Roy Brown was directing operations, but because that's the way things seemed to work at Ford in those days. Gradually, however, favoured features included a long tapering flute along the flanks (though the dihedral rear-end style approved in November 1960 was then thrown out in January 1961, when John Bugas of Ford-International visited

Dagenham and objected to what he saw).

'So we end up with those "ban the bomb" lights instead,' Hamish Orr-Ewing remembers, 'which caused all sort of snide remarks, including the question "Is this a Mercedes-Benz, upside down?" – but they were good, low cost and *very* visible tail lamps.'

The style of the front end also became a real bone of contention: 'The original car we put forward as the "Base" model had a rather

blank grille as part of the sheet metal, because the whole object was to keep the costs down. We wanted a neat car, and not a "tin crocodile," and although there was quite a considerable clash of cultures between the various visitors, Roy Brown did a very good job of matching American ideas to European ideas, and steered the thing through pretty well.'

Engineering design

Although the style of the new car was still under discussion, its engineering was going ahead. Settling on the main mechanical elements was straightforward enough – all were evolutions of the successful new Anglia 105E layout, as we shall see. Much of the innovation went into the engineering of the body shell itself.

Here, for the first time, Ford set out to develop a shell which was as light as possible for the job it had to do. The two key engineers were Don Ward, Ford's Australian-born Chief Body Engineer, and Dennis Roberts, who had spent time with the Bristol Aeroplane Company before settling at Briggs Motor Bodies, the shell-making subsidiary which had been absorbed into Ford-UK in 1958.

Don Ward wanted to use the skills of an engineer familiar with the theoretical side of body construction:

'I had this unique background,' Roberts once said, 'of being trained as an automobile engineer and an

The Ford MacPherson strut suspension was simple and effective. First seen on the original Consul/Zephyr of 1950, it would then be used on all other new British Ford cars announced in the 1950s and 1960s.

Starting in 1959, Ford invested heavily in a new family of four-cylinder engines which would be pivotal to the success of the new Cortina range. Although they looked simple enough, they proved exceptionally tuneable.

aircraft stressman.' This explains why Ward allocated him the body engineering job, telling him he wanted to see a structure as much as 150lb lighter than that of the Classic!

There were no computers to help in those days, but by applying aircraft stressing principles and techniques, by reducing the number of pressings by 20 per cent, and by removing metal where it wasn't needed, the job was eventually done.

David Burgess-Wise, who saw the results of all this at Ford, recently wrote that: 'The complex sums which ensured that the Cortina body shell combined maximum strength and lightness were performed by ... Dennis Roberts, who covered hundreds of sheets of paper with his calculations.'

One way in which weight could be reduced was to make one component do more than one job – which explains why there was no boot floor pressing above the original petrol tank!

After years of experience with the systems, Raviolo's team readily opted for MacPherson strut front suspension, allied to recirculating ball steering, and eventually for simple, basic half-elliptic leaf springs to suspend *and locate* the beam rear axle.

There were qualms, however, especially as the forthcoming BMC 1100 was sure to have independent rear suspension, and a system inspired from Detroit was actually considered at first, though finally rejected in May 1961 before serious testing had begun.

Those who suggested this would produce a car with poor handling were soon shamed into silence, when Cortina GTs started to perform so well in races and rallies. That silence was positively deafening from 1965, when the same system – aided only by radius arms at the rear – proved to be more effective than the

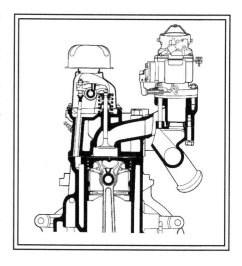

The original Cortina engine was a simple and rugged four-cylinder unit, with pushrod overhead-valve operation, 'bathtub' combustion chambers and a downdraught carburettor. From late 1967 it would be replaced by the definitive bowl-in-piston 'Kent' engine (see page 38).

Right and below: Two versions of the same engine/ transmission assembly, as used in the original Cortinas. Most British-market cars had the centre floor gearchange, but a steering-column change, using cables between the gearbox and the steering column, was also available.

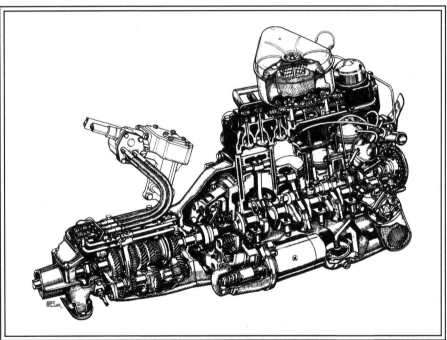

original (and more sophisticated) Lotus-Cortina layout ...

Although the engines and transmissions of the Anglia 105E/ Classic 109E family were used as a basis for the new car's drive-line, both were changed considerably.

Engine

The 1340cc unit as used in the Classic 109E, when revved hard was quite a rough engine, but this did not initially worry Terry Beckett and Hamish Orr-Ewing as they needed less than 50bhp for the entry-level version of the new car, and settled for a 1198cc engine size which had a shorter stroke than the 1340cc, and felt smoother.

'We started off with the 1200 version,' Hamish Orr-Ewing says, 'and initially this was the only version we intended to produce. Our first proposals never even mentioned 1500s, and certainly not 1500GTs.'

Theoretically, that was as far as the capacity could be stretched, and engine design chief Alan Worters (described by one erstwhile colleague as 'an arrogant and unattractive personality') was reluctant to try for more.

He had a point, for without deepening the cylinder block there simply was no way to make the engine larger, and that solution was going to cost millions in modifying the production line transfer machinery. Money, as we now know, was eventually found. A five-bearing

bottom end was developed – once again, Worters originally said it was 'impossible to do,' but was persuaded otherwise – the cylinder block was deepened by 16.8mm/0.66in, the crankshaft throw lengthened by 3.86mm/0.15in ... the result was a new swept volume of 1498cc.

Transmission

Similarly, transmission expert

Alf Haig masterminded a gearbox change. As introduced for the Anglia 105E/Classic 109E, this new component was a compact gearbox without synchromesh on first gear. To match the new 1498cc engine (and also the 1198cc unit) it was redesigned to incorporate synchromesh on first gear, but because this added length and bulk to the assembly, a new casing was needed, longer than before by 4.83mm/0.19in:

'Alf Haig agonised about this,' Orr-Ewing recalls, 'because he also had to narrow the other gear teeth to get them in the casing. The company's standard, I believe, was 100,000lb/sq.in of tooth loading, and he went to all sorts of pains. He'd found by experience that if this was exceeded, you would begin to get tooth failures in extreme conditions ...'

That change is reputed to have cost an extra £750,000 in investment capital, which gives a fair idea of the pressures under which the Beckett/Orr-Ewing/Hart/Worters team was operating.

Both steering column and centre floor gearchanges were developed. Surveys showed that while 95 per cent of British customers wanted a floor change, only 40 per cent of overseas customers thought the same. Since it was intended to sell the new 'Archbishop' all over the world, both systems were clearly necessary.

At first, Ford did not consider specifying automatic transmission as an option – the marketplace, it was thought, was not actually crying out for such a fitting on a car of this price, and in any case there was no suitable 'off-the-shelf' transmission which could be bought in.

Two years later that situation would have changed, because Borg Warner (from a factory in Letchworth) was about to launch the three-speed Type 35 automatic. BMC was its first major customer – offering the box on most of its medium-sized cars – and Ford would eventually follow suit in 1964 (but only for the Cortina 1500).

What's in a name?

One major problem facing Ford in the early months of 1962 was to decide on a product name for the 'Archbishop.' Well before the project had been defined (before the German 'Cardinal' had arrived to muddy the water) there was talk of developing a new 'Prefect,' but that idea was soon ditched when the new car evolved into a much bigger machine.

Harry Calton, one-time office boy in the Public Affairs department, but more recently getting involved in preparations for launching the new car, told me that: 'We did the photography of the first Cortinas in March 1962. I was sent up to Scotland by Walter Hayes with three cars – two two-door saloons and a four-door.

'The four-door didn't actually work, but was a "design property" which had to be moved around, not driven around. We had a "design" man with us who could put back on all the bits that tended to fall off!

'We took them up to Scotland in furniture vans. We got very clever because we also rented Vauxhall Victors, so that if we were found, everyone would think we were photographing new Vauxhalls!

'At the time, the new car was going to be called Consul 225 with a 1200 engine, and the 1500 was going to be a Consul 255. We were in Scotland for three weeks, and for the first two-and-a-half of those weeks we photographed cars with Consul 225/255 badges.

'Then I got a telegram saying that there had been a late change, and that "Edgy" Fabris, who was my boss, was coming to Scotland, and with some new badges. We then had to re-photograph as much as

In comparison with the new Cortina, the third-generation Zephyr/Zodiac family – also born in 1962 – was an old-style Ford, very heavy and rather transatlantic in appearance.

we could in two-and-a-half days with new Cortina badges. There was some stuff we couldn't redo, but we managed to find enough from them which didn't actually show the badges ...'

As we all know, the car was finally launched as the 'Consul Cortina' – but why 'Cortina,' and why 'Consul'?

Terry Beckett had put together a long list of possible names, trying them out on everyone he could find. Walter Hayes, who had recently arrived at Ford as the Director of Public Affairs, remembers that:

'Sir Patrick Hennessy didn't like any of them at first. I went into his office one day, and Pat read out names, and they all sounded unsuitable ...'

Somehow, though, 'Cortina' was chosen, deriving from the Italian ski resort, Cortina d'Ampezzo, which had recently been the site of the 1960 Winter Olympics – the name therefore added a fashionable sporting sparkle to the product. It also helped locate the new car's marketing image in Europe rather than in the UK, which appealed to Sir Patrick Hennessy's desire to fight

back at Ford-Germany. (Somehow, there was no question of calling it the 'Consul Clapton,' 'Consul Colchester,' or whatever!)

It wasn't until later that Walter Hayes discovered that 'cortina' means 'curtains' in Spanish – but at least he had the grace to contact the authorities in Cortina to ask them if they minded that their name be used on a new Ford car.

'After it was agreed, we promised them that we would eventually take some cars and some Ford personalities there for some publicity visits.'

When the Cortina came to the end of its twenty-year career, and an affectionate TV programme was written about the car, comedian Alexei Sayle said he thought Terry Beckett had chosen that name because he had been buying his lunch from a local Italian sandwich bar called "Cortina" ...

The continued use of 'Consul' in the title was always a puzzle, for no-one outside Ford ever seemed to use it or take any notice of it. Perhaps there was the desire to link it, in some way, to existing Consul models but:

'I suspect Patrick Hennessy was emotionally attached to it,' Hamish Orr-Ewing thinks, 'and I think Ford just wanted to keep using one of its trademark names, and in the end it became a habit.'

Even so, public indifference soon overcame this attitude. Although the first Cortinas had a 'Consul' badge on the bonnet, at the nose of the pressing bulge, once the car got its mid-term facelift in October 1964, that badge was re-titled 'Cortina' instead. Thereafter, as far as this car was concerned, the 'Consul' name was discarded, never to be restored.

Design – basic design, that is, rather than detail refinement – was completed by the end of 1960, and development got under way rapidly in 1961: it had to, for Sir Patrick Hennessy was determined to see the very first 'off-tools' cars built in June 1962. Pilot production cars, in other words, were to be produced before the annual summer holiday 'shutdown,' and he was also determined to get thousands of cars out to the dealers before the end of September, when the car was due to be launched.

Launching the original Cortina in front of hard-bitten Ford dealers. Richard Martindale is on the microphone, and the cutaway model shows off the passenger box and huge boot.

Along the way there was a change of emphasis, and just one important specification change – one more concerned with aesthetics than function. Hamish Orr-Ewing remembers why:

'At first, nothing was considered bar the basic car, for there was to be a Standard and a De Luxe model, with tarted up trim, stripes, that sort of thing. The 1500 Super only came into being after the five-bearing engine became available – it was a good engineer called Ken Teesdale, with the blessing of Fred Hart, who made that possible.'

Visually the bone of contention was the original fascia style:

'The early panel was very stark and very crude,' says Terry Beckett. 'The real problem was I was insisting that we kept it down to the planned cost. Well, to be honest, our original objectives were too tight....

'I remember Pat Hennessy and I looking at it, and it was just he and I together, and he said : "Terry, it's a bit bare," but I persuaded him we had to meet the planned costs. So he supported me on that, he supported me all the way through.

'It was too late to alter the car (which went on sale at the end of 1962) but within a year (and from the start on the Lotus-Cortina) it was updated:

'The original was down to my lack of understanding of public demand,' Orr-Ewing admits. 'The instrument panel was regarded as too minimalist; there were

considerable changes made, but it did put up costs quite a lot.

'Then I had the idea of using a binnacle instrument panel which left one with a very uncluttered and very simple low-cost dashboard. There was also the simple stalk device on which one had the indicator switch – I and my colleagues found absolutely no problem in using this at all, but it was very unpopular.'

Behind the scenes, Dagenham's long-suffering production engineers faced yet another upheaval. In preparation for all this, Dagenham had been treated to a totally new paint, trim and assembly plant, with improved links from the press shop – much of the expense being incurred in the late 1950s when the company was by no means profitable. It needed a steadfast boss of Sir Patrick Hennessy's calibre to push it all through and stand up to the trans-Atlantic 'bean counters' who wanted to know where all the money was going.

Sir Terence Beckett smiles about it these days, but at the time it all looked very serious:

'I can remember everyone going

round saying that this really had put Ford back by a generation. It was complete doom and gloom – we actually cut parts of that building to save money where, had we continued with the original plan, we would have had more capacity.

'What we actually did was to open things up on a piecemeal basis, which wasn't ideal. It wasn't ideal from a cost point of view either.'

[In 1997, as I write this chapter, I notice that yet another extension of that massive building is taking place ...]

In the foregoing years, the first truly major product change at Dagenham had come in 1959, when the all-new Anglia 105E appeared, with new body structure, new engine and new transmission – an enormous investment and quickly followed by the arrival of the Classic 109E in May 1961.

Now, for 1962, the planners were faced with not one but several major launches, one being the arrival of the Mk III edition of the Zephyr/Zodiac range; other events included new machining plant to build the five-bearing version of the Cortina's engine, along with

In the late 1950s, Ford began a major expansion at Dagenham, the most important element being the £75 million paint, trim and assembly plant close to the A13 road. The Anglia 105E was the first all-new car to be built there, with the Cortina following in 1962.

the latest all-synchromesh gearbox. The Cortina introduction completed the rush.

Even so, as Hamish Orr-Ewing recalls, it *was* achieved:

'Ford was always solid, methodical and sound, and things just *had* to happen when planned. Job One of the Cortina came down the line on schedule on 4 June 1962, which is when it had always been scheduled. I remember Stan Rees, who was head of the Assembly Division at the time, telling me how

his people had pulled out every stop in the world to achieve that.

'We really did build a lot of cars before the official launch date. There were cars in every dealership on the day we announced the car, which I believe was unique for those days, nobody had ever done that before.'

Harry Calton confirms this: 'I think what worked best for the Cortina was that they were always available – you couldn't buy Morris 1100s at the time. The weekend we

launched, every British dealer had between twelve and fifteen motor cars – and they were ready to sell them. Every dealer knew that by the next weekend he was going to have another fifteen cars! It had never happened before, not even at Ford. Previously, we had launched cars and the first ones had all gone for export.'

But this was only the start. Next – would the public take to the new car?

2

CORTINA I AND II MILLION SELLERS

Introducing the Cortina was less about launching a new car than an entirely new Ford Motor Company. Well before the new model was ready to go on sale, Sir Patrick Hennessy had decided to remodel the image of the colossus he had been astride for so long. First the Cortina, then the whole company.

The man he chose to do this for him was Walter Hayes. The Hayes legend is well known at Ford, and has been carved, refined and embellished over the years. Hayes himself insists that he was merely the head of a great new team, but there is no doubt that his inspiration got the job done.

A journalist by profession, he had risen to dizzy heights in the *Daily Mail* by 1961: he saw everyone, knew everyone, lunched and dined with the great, the good and the powerful – including Ford's Chairman. Sir Patrick Hennessy was about to hire a new Managing Director – Yorkshireman Alan Barke – and thought he might need guidance:

'Sir Patrick Hennessy asked me

The original 'base' Cortina – the least expensive of the type – had this simple radiator grille style when launched in 1962.

to lunch,' Hayes told me, 'and made it clear he thought that Ford-UK was still far too much an introspective multinational company, and that it needed to be woken up to the kind of world that was developing. He thought he needed somebody on the Board who really knew something about politics, the way the world was changing, social movements and all the rest ...'

That was the Good Idea but the result was rather different. Realising that the only way to change Ford's image was to change its image-makers, Sir Patrick hired Hayes as his Director of Public Affairs, with a very broad brief. Arriving at the end of 1961, his immediate concern was the launch of the Zephyr / Zodiac Mk III – and after that, the Cortina:

'When I got to Dagenham, the Cortina was coming to the end of its development stage, so one had a lot of time to

As Terry Beckett always insisted, the Cortina needed a vast boot to make it attractive and this proved to be true. (Incidentally, the petrol tank is hidden under the indentation in the floor mat.)

think about this car, which was clearly going to be an important new model.'

Because he was effectively replacing the legendary figure of Colonel Buckmaster, the World War 2 hero who had run Ford's public relations department for so long, Hayes knew he would be under the spotlight and played it cool for a time.

'Walter then arrived,' Harry Calton told me, 'but we weren't told much. This small man arrived and sat in his corner office with his typewriter. He then started to hire people – he'd obviously been given a clean sheet of paper. As he once told me afterwards, he had no budget

The original Cortina was introduced with the word 'CONSUL' emblazoned on the bonnet badge: this would give way to 'CORTINA' at 'face-lift' time. This was the Super model, introduced in January 1963.

The Corsair, introduced in 1963, was based on a longer wheelbase version of the Cortina's platform, but with a completely different body superstructure.

Corsair – kissing cousin

Without the Cortina there would have been no Corsair. This sharp-nosed Ford of the 1960s looked completely different to the Cortina – and was always priced and marketed that important bit further upmarket. Yet there was a lot of Cortina engineering under the skin.

'We needed a replacement for the Classic,' Sir Terence Beckett recalls,' and we thought an extension of the Cortina was a way of doing this.

'I think it was a very useful stopgap – it wasn't an extensive one to do; there was a lot of commonality with the Cortina.'

The Corsair was introduced in October 1963, and was the first Ford production car to be built in the brand-new Halewood plant on Merseyside. Although its styling was definitely inspired by the latest Ford-USA Thunderbird, it was based on a slightly stretched Cortina Mk I platform, engine, transmission and suspension.

The car was rather painstakingly titled the 'Consul Corsair' (if you forget the 'Consul' part, Ford will surely forgive you – they forgot, too!). It ran on a 101in/3565mm wheelbase, which was exactly three inches longer than that of the Cortina. The entire floorpan, scuttle/bulkhead, windscreen, inner engine bay panels and related hardware were all Cortina-based, the actual 'stretch' being in the rear compartment where the floorpan was lengthened to give more rear-seat leg room. Two-door and four-door types were immediately available.

Original Corsairs used Cortina 1500GT suspensions – front and rear tracks, brakes and steering were all shared. There was a choice of 59.5bhp (Cortina 1500 Super) or 78bhp (Cortina GT) engines, with the same gearbox, but a choice of steering-column or floor change (the remote-control floor change was standard on the Corsair GT). The same Borg Warner Type 35 automatic transmission became optional on Cortinas and Corsairs.

This is how the prices of the different Cortina and Corsair two-door and four-door cars lined up in the 1963-64 UK market:

Cortina 1500 Super....................	£688
Corsair 1500 De Luxe................	£701
Cortina GT................................	£767
Corsair GT................................	£840

Thereafter the Corsair rapidly developed its own personality. From the autumn of 1965, the Cortina engines were dropped in favour of two completely new 60-degree V4s – a 76.5bhp/1699cc and an 88bhp/1996cc example – with a change of model name to Corsair V4 and Corsair 2000.

From the spring of 1966 an estate car version of the 2000 was added to the range: this car was actually a factory-approved conversion by Abbotts of Farnham, from partly built saloons.

From January 1967 an even more upmarket derivative, the 2000E saloon, was added to the range, this being a near-100mph machine with a 97bhp/1996cc version of the V4 engine, a much better set of internal gear ratios – as was soon found in the Cortina GT Mk II – radial-ply tyres, a vinyl roof covering and a very glossy interior.

From mid-1969 Corsair assembly was transferred from Halewood to Dagenham to allow more space for more Capris to be built at Halewood. The last cars of all were produced at Dagenham in June 1970, only a few weeks before the 'donor car' – the Cortina Mk II – also dropped out of production.

In seven years, a total of 331,095 Corsairs were built, of which 31,566 were 2000Es but only 940 were estate cars. Because the Cortina III was a rather larger car than the Cortina II – with more interior space, in particular, than before – it also took over from the Corsair, so this model name went back into Ford's reserve and has never been used in the UK again.

and no direction, so therefore he followed his own instincts.'

The first major change was to the way in which new models were to be launched:

'When Buckmaster launched the Anglia 105E, we had properly prepared 'press cars,' and actually took over Crystal Palace race circuit for two days, and finally the press were allowed in.

'Walter arrived and we then launched the new Zephyr/Zodiacs at Silverstone – not much change there.

'With the Cortina, though, it was all going to be different. When the advertising was being prepared, it was probably the first time we used what you would probably call "lifestyle" photography. We hired models that looked like mums and dads and their children. We did the picnic scene, we did all the things a family would be seen to do.'

Then, for the first time, Hayes decided to bring press and new car together indoors in a plushy atmosphere, choosing to do this at London's Grosvenor House hotel. Not only were there cars on stage and on show, but some were sectioned to show off technical novelties, and Ford management (with Hamish Orr-Ewing taking a big part) gave carefully choreographed presentations.

There were only four, slightly different Cortinas in the range which was revealed to the public in September 1962. All had 48.5bhp/1.2-litre engines, and all had four-speed all-synchromesh transmissions, available in two-door or four-door, Standard or De Luxe form. At the time no-one could have realised (and Ford was not telling ...) that this range was to expand mightily over the next two years.

The launch was a glossy occasion carefully stage-managed, but as a drum-beating exercise it was only partially successful. Knowing that it would be difficult to convince the press about the ultra-light construction housing a conventional layout, the company banged the advertising drum for 'The Small Car with the Big Difference.'

When the new car finally met its public, the press gave it a decidedly mixed reception. Not only had the media been thoroughly seduced by the cheeky attractions of the Mini and 1100 in recent years, but they found it difficult to get excited about Ford's new Cortina when, to them, its only obvious selling points were lightness, mechanical simplicity, a roomy cabin and good value for money.

Ford's own dealers were concerned about the newspaper comments, and were especially frightened by the enthusiastic reception given a few weeks earlier to the technologically advanced front-wheel-drive BMC 1100.

They need not have worried; before the end of the year, the Cortina had started to sell in large numbers, not only to thrifty private buyers but, very gratifyingly, to the burgeoning fleet market.

Autocar magazine's reception

The original Cortina was available as a two-door saloon (this car), four-door saloon and five-door estate car.

One version of the Cortina Mark I estate car had large imitation-wood panels along the flanks.

was typical: 'Unorthodoxy is not a virtue in itself, and the creators of the Cortina were fully aware of what was germinating elsewhere on the Ford tree.'

[This was an obvious reference to the arrival of the front-wheel-drive Ford-Germany Taunus 12M.]

'... the term conventional should certainly not be construed to imply lack of development, for the Cortina results from an intensive study, backed by long experience, of what the great majority of motorists want and need ...'

Even so, there was dismay – implicit rather than spelled out – at the basic specification. Drum brakes all round (the Morris 1100 had front discs), a beam axle rear suspension (the 1100 had independent rear suspension) and no other interesting features (like a transverse engine, front-wheel-drive or hydrolastic springing) all made the dealer chain wonder if it would sell any cars at all ... until they saw the prices.

The table below shows how the original Cortina was priced in the UK, compared with its most important rivals.

On the Cortina, incidentally, the steering-column gearchange (along with a front bench seat to match) cost an extra £13.75. Other extras included a heater (£17.19), leather upholstery (£17.19) and two-tone paintwork for just £6.88.

All these prices were lowered from mid-November 1962, when purchase tax was reduced. From that moment Cortina prices started at a mere £573.

The new Cortina clearly offered remarkable value, being cheaper than any of its rivals and offering a larger cabin, lighter weight and (potentially) better fuel economy.

Within months, expansion of the range got under way and the 1500 Super and five-door estate car types both arrived in the first months of 1963 – although

overshadowed, inevitably, by the premature launch of the Lotus-Cortina (which I describe more fully in Chapter 3).

The Super combined the latest five-bearing 60bhp/1.5-litre engine and higher gearing, with a higher quality of trim and equipment (though no disc brakes at this stage), while the estate car was a workmanlike five-door derivative of the saloon car's layout, complete with a fold-flat rear seat and (for the Super) acres of plastic 'wood' panelling along the flanks.

The options then started to get really complicated. Not only were Supers available as two-door or four-door saloons, but the 1498cc engine was then offered as an extra in the De Luxe saloons,

This was the detail of the original Cortina estate car, showing how the rear seat cushion could be somersaulted forward to provide yet more loading space behind the front seats.

Cortina 1200 2-door Standard	**£639**
Cortina 1200 4-door Standard	**£660**
Cortina 1200 2-door De Luxe	**£667**
Morris 1100 4-door	£675
Morris 1100 4-door De Luxe	£695
Vauxhall Victor (1.5 litres)	£702
Vauxhall Victor Super (1.5 litres)	£737
Vauxhall Victor De Luxe (1.5 litres)	£799
Cortina 1200 4-door De Luxe	**£687**
Hillman Minx 1600	£702

The Mk I estate car was always a great success: light, versatile and very capacious.

and the estate cars could either be to 1200 De Luxe or 1500 Super specification.

To give the new Super's image an immediate boost, Walter Hayes sent Eric Jackson and Ken Chambers to drive from London to Cape Town in record time. Taking a route by way of ferry to Tunis, they sped on to Cairo and Nairobi, reaching Cape Town in 13 days 8 hours and 48 minutes, which was just 18 minutes faster than the previous record.

Then in April came the best new Cortina so far – the original Cortina GT. Launched months after the Lotus-Cortina, but available well before it and donating some of its chassis equipment to that car, but having its own robust 1.5-litre engine, it was a great car, soon recognised as such by enthusiasts. Yes – I ordered one in 1964, enjoyed every minute of it and then replaced it with a 1966 model!

In many ways the Cortina GT

was the result of an inspired bit of Walter Hayes whimsy. Just before the new Cortina and the Taunus 12M were introduced, Ford set up a marketing conference, and hired the Montlhéry race track near Paris. Here, they arranged a big line-up of pilot-built Cortinas and Taunus 12Ms, along with some of their obvious European rivals, and encouraged every Ford mandarin, from Henry Ford II downwards, to assess what was about to go on sale.

Then, as later, there was great rivalry between Ford-UK and Ford-Germany:

'There was some discussion about what we should do,' Walter Hayes told me. 'I remember talking to Fred Hart, and

The route chosen by Ford for the London to Cape Town record run in a Cortina, early in 1963.

The Cortina that accomplished the London to Cape Town record run in 1963, before its hammering across the deserts and scrub lands began. Eric Jackson and Ken Chambers shared the driving.

he was going on about having a "secret weapon." I'm not quite sure about the final idea, but Fred's team already had a 105E engine with twin carburettors. We decided that we had to have something like that for the Cortina, but we needed to have a badge, to call it something. There's a legendary story, which may even be true, that Fred sent someone round to Halfords, and the only pretty badge he could find was one which said "GT" ...

'When we got out to the race track, Henry Ford looked at the car, and said to Fred Hart: "What's that?" Fred replied that it wasn't ready for production, but that we were thinking of doing it.

' "Can I drive it?", Henry said – which was exactly what we'd wanted him to do. Now Henry liked to go quickly, so he blew absolutely everything else out of the way, came back and said: "You must build that!", so Fred assumed that this was official approval.

'Everyone then returned to England, not so much obsessed with the car, but with the fact that they'd won their first European Championship against Ford-Germany.'

All this, and an early request from Ford-Australia (which would be building Cortinas from kits supplied from Dagenham) helped crystallise the specification of the 118E GT. Hamish Orr-Ewing told me how:

'Geelong [where cars were manufactured in Australia] sent over a very tough and capable engineer so that he could help develop a much more robust body/chassis structure, particularly around the top of the MacPherson struts. That provided the opportunity for putting the 1500 engine in it, with uprated brakes and a compound double-choke Weber carburettor.'

The Cortina GT came together at an enormous pace and was launched at the start of April 1963, with deliveries beginning almost at once. Those were the days when

The London to Cape Town record car at top speed, in Africa, on its dash to Cape Town.

28

Launching the Cortina in Paris in June 1962 at the Montlhéry track. Cortinas share the line-up with Taunus 12Ms and competing models.

Henry Ford (left) and Fred Hart with the prototype Cortina GT – the 'secret weapon' hastily built for the Montlhéry launch.

'You must build that!' declared Henry Ford, following his first drive in the prototype Cortina GT.

I was Ford dealer Phil Simister's regular rallying co-driver. Up to that point we had been using a 1498cc-engined Anglia, but we started using a brand-new Cortina GT before midsummer, as soon as a few necessary bits had been sourced from Boreham.

Boosting the 1.5-litre engine's power to 78bhp had been achieved with help from Cosworth Engineering (whose miraculous tuning jobs on the 105E engine had already made it the most successful Formula Junior power unit):

'We produced the camshaft for that,' Cosworth founder Keith Duckworth says, 'and an inlet manifold – the two-ring type of manifold which had a Weber carburettor sitting on it ... we introduced Ford to Weber carbs. In the end I sold the design of the GT camshaft to Ford for £750. Incidentally, I was very surprised that Ford cleared our cam to run up to 6000rpm, for I could hear it surging, quite clearly, at about 5800rpm...

The Cortina GT, first seen in the spring of 1963, was a 95mph machine with front disc brakes. The car immediately found its place in races and rallies.

Billed at the time as 'Stirling Moss's Dream Car,' this was a two-door Cortina restyled by Ogle Design. It was a one-off.

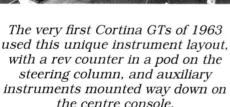

The very first Cortina GTs of 1963 used this unique instrument layout, with a rev counter in a pod on the steering column, and auxiliary instruments mounted way down on the centre console.

The original very stark instrument panel was abandoned after only one year and replaced by this neat but still simple layout with circular dials. This was a 1500 Super model of 1964, with optional automatic transmission.

selling as fast as the much-feared Morris 1100. Sir Patrick Hennessy's gamble, it seems, had paid off. By midsummer, with prices spanning £573 (1200 Standard 2-door) to £767 (1500GT 4-door) there seemed to be a Cortina for everyone.

Changes then followed thick and fast, for in spite of Terry Beckett's insistence on meeting costs, something had to be done about the fascia/control layout. From September 1963 the lacklustre 109E Classic was dropped, which cleared the showrooms of two outwardly rather similar cars, while at the same time all Cortinas were treated to a new fascia, with the strip-type speedometer abandoned in favour of a binnacle containing all the instruments, the GT no longer needing a pod for its rev counter. Then, from the end of the year, Ford finally introduced Borg Warner Type 35 automatic transmission as an option on 60bhp/1.5-litre models only.

The first major change for all models came in October 1964.

To go with the new engine Ford added a remote-control gearchange inside a centre console, front-wheel disc brakes, larger rear brakes, stiffer suspension, a rev counter mounted in a pod on the steering column and extra auxiliary dials on the centre console. Once again, two-door or four-door saloons were available. Some people still think the Cortina GT raided the Lotus-Cortina 'parts bin' for some of its chassis and transmission – but it was actually the other way round, as the Cortina GT was already being developed when the Lotus-Cortina was conceived.

By this time the UK range of Cortinas had been expanded to eleven models (though the Lotus-Cortina was still not really in series production) and it was already

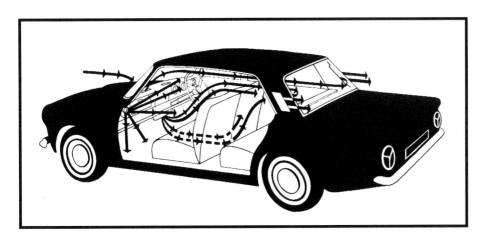

At 'facelift' time, October 1964, Ford made much of the new face-level ventilation system, which was certainly a 'first' as far as saloon cars were concerned.

Facelift Cortina Mk Is with aeroflow ventilation were fitted with this, the third Cortina fascia style introduced in two years. GT versions had extra instruments mounted above the radio installation.

Although we did not know it at the time, Ford was already committed to what it called a 'four-year cycle' for the Cortina family. In Product Planning terms this meant that a completely new body style would be introduced after four years, and in addition there would be a mid-life 'makeover' after only two years.

In October 1964, therefore, the Cortina received a completely new fascia style – its third in two years! – along with the undoubted advance of face-level ventilation. The fascia now featured cowled circular instruments in a new pressing (which, obviously, was 'handed' right or left depending on the steering position) with auxiliary instruments positioned in the centre for GT models.

Ford called the new ventilation system 'Aeroflow.' It featured swivelling 'eyeball' face-level vents at each side of the fascia panel, with louvred extractor vents in the rear panels alongside the rear window. Face-level air might not have been a world's first (Triumph got there in 1961 on the TR4 sportscar) but it immediately made the Cortina the best-ventilated family car in Europe, if not in the world.

At the same time engine compression ratios were raised from 8.3:1 to 9.0:1, front-wheel disc brakes were standardised on all models, there was a new and more stylish grille, 'CORTINA' took over from 'CONSUL' on the bonnet badge, and for GT models a pair of trailing radius arms was added inboard of the leaf springs, to control rear axle movements.

Management upheavals brought Allan Barke even more responsibility as Managing Director (Sir Patrick Hennessy, still Chairman, was moving smoothly towards retirement) while Terry Beckett finally moved out of Product Planning to take over as Marketing Manager.

Not that the Cortina needed much marketing – to sell adequate numbers of cars anyway – for demand had always exceeded original forecasts. One of Beckett's immediate responsibilities was to see that the desired types continued to reach dealers in appropriate quantities:

'There's no doubt about it, it was a good car to sell. Though it had to be accompanied by all the right sort of aids, we did a tremendous

The Cortina Super could always be recognised by the chrome strips along the flanks, defining the crease of the body shape.

job with the dealers in the 1960s, people really don't understand how much.

'Even by then many of them were in the third or fourth generation of one family. But I wasn't at all satisfied with the performance we were getting from some of our dealers. We had to get rid of an awful lot of retail dealers – a lot of them weren't devoted entirely to Ford, they were selling other makes too.

'Next we divided the UK up into four hundred areas, and in those areas we determined what share of the market they should be getting; then, if they were not, we went into each dealership and told them what had got to happen, sometimes it meant they had to get rid of their old premises.

'The opposition hadn't ever done this – the effectiveness was in replacing some defective dealers. I had to make a lot of visits – sometimes I had to go in to a dealer and thump on his desk. I had some terrible problems ...'

In 1965 and 1966 though the Cortina was continually reaching new peaks, bustling past them and aiming even higher. As one new option appeared, an unsuccessful type might be abandoned: the stark '1200 Standard' saloon was

The Cortina was given a facelift package from 1964, which included a new wider front grille, and the word 'CORTINA' on the bonnet badge.

To help keep its rear axle in check, the Cortina GT was provided with twin trailing radius arms, which would feature on all GTs until 1968 (when they were gradually phased out).

dropped in September 1965, and at the same time the steering-column option was dropped. The front quarter windows became fixed (with Aeroflow ventilation, forced flow through the quarter windows wasn't needed any more) and the simulated wood on the flanks of the Super estate car was discontinued.

The millionth Cortina was built in September 1966, which at the time made it the fastest selling British Ford ever. Ford also pointed out that the Cortina was the first British Ford to achieve £250 million

Ford took many of its famous race and rally drivers to join the fun in Cortina, celebrating the 'Car of the Year' award. Among those in this group are Eric Jackson, Bo Ljungfeldt, Gilbert Staepelaere, Jack Sears and Jim Clark.

Tens of thousands of Ford enthusiasts (I was one) bought Cortina GTs in the mid-1960s. This was the 1964-66 'facelift' variety, which was available in two-door or four-door styles. This particular car has the optional 4.5J wide-rim wheels.

in export earnings – and that it was Britain's most exported car of all.

Could Ford do better in future? With a new body style, it thought it could.

Cortina Mk II – new style, same chassis

Well before the introduction of the first 'mid-term' facelift, work at

33

Hail and farewell – one of the last Mk Is passes a new Cortina Mk II at announcement time in 1966.

Ford had already started on the next-generation car. There was to be a phased launch of Cortina Mark IIs, first seen in October 1966 (on the eve of the London Motor Show). The first of these cars featured little more than a new body style, with the definitive 'bowl-in-piston' (BIP) engines following a year later.

Although Ford had already sold more than a million of the original Cortina, there seemed to be no question of developing an all-new car to succeed it. Deciding that the vast majority of its customers never looked under the bonnet of a Ford – and certainly never looked at the underside and the running gear – the company elected to retain the existing platform and running gear and build a new shell around it.

Like the original car, the Mark II had a 98-inch wheelbase and was almost exactly 168 inches long, but from that point the before-and-after dimensions began to diverge. Compared with the original, the Mark II had a front track three inches wider, a body shell 2.4 inches wider, and a rather more roomy cabin. It was no wonder, therefore, that the new car was advertised under the headline: 'New Cortina is more Cortina.'

For the Mark II, in fact, the complex steel pressings making up the 'chassis' platform/underframe, the engine bay area and all the mountings for the suspension, steering, engine and transmission, had all been retained. The petrol

The Mark II Cortina used the same platform as the Mark I, but with a different superstructure.

tank had been enlarged to a capacity of 10 gallons/45.5 litres.

Above that, all was fresh and new. The new body looked completely different to the original Cortina – rounded where the original had been craggy, plump rather than rakish, and somehow with less immediately recognisable character. At the time – 1966-67 – it didn't help the Cortina Mark II's cause that it looked very similar to the new Hillman Hunter (which was launched at the same Motor Show). [I have talked to Rootes/Hillman stylists, too, and both groups of designers insist they had

no foreknowledge of the other car, and that there was no question of copying either way.]

Although there were some styling cues from the same Ford studio which had shaped the recently launched Zephyr/Zodiac Mark IV, the bonnet/cabin/tail shape was much better balanced. In comparison with the earlier Cortina, too, there seemed to be a larger glass area. As expected, two-door and four-door saloons were launched at once, and the five-door estate car version followed in February 1967.

The new design had, in some

ways, a more integrated theme than that of the first Cortina, with a full-width front grille incorporating side/indicator lamps, and with rear lamp clusters wrapped around the corners. As before, different brightwork graced different derivatives, wheel trims on the original GT looked like those of the larger Fords, and at first the front door opening quarterlights were fitted only to export cars.

The big improvement was to the interior, where there was a smooth new fascia/instrument panel layout; on the GT the extra instruments were positioned high in the crash roll, above the heater controls. Incidentally, this was the fourth distinctly different fascia style to be employed in only four

years. There would be a bit more stability after this change, but version four-and-a-half came along only two years later!

Compared to the 1964-66 variety, the Aeroflow face-level ventilation system had been refined, giving 25 per cent more through-flow of air. (The opposition – having studied what Ford had done in 1964 – was now catching up, so further improvements were necessary.)

Blatant Americanisms, like bench front seats and steering column gearchange, had virtually been eliminated – in any case, there was little customer demand for either of these features. All Mark IIs now had

centre floor gearchanges (the GT with a modified type of linkage). A steering column change was still available on export Mk IIs, but I have never seen such a car in the UK. A front bench was only available as an option on the 1500 Super. All other cars were fitted with separate front seats; on the four-door Super and GT types reclining front seats were also optional.

Because the body had been bulked out, the front and rear tracks

The Mark II GT originally had this well-stocked fascia/instrument panel.

The Mark II was launched in 1966, with 1.3-litre, 1.5-litre and 1.5-litre GT engine options. This was the 1.3-litre De Luxe derivative.

For the Cortina Mk II Ford developed a new type of remote-control centre gearshift, standard on the GT from late 1966 and added to the Super model later.

could be increased to suit. At the front there were longer track control arms, a different anti-roll bar, and slightly realigned MacPherson struts, the result being a three inch track increase and a reduction in roll centre height; at the rear the axle tubes were lengthened to give a track of 51.0in.

Not only that but the chassis engineers had completely revised the suspension settings, softening up the front springs from 100lb/in to 74lb/in on the mass-market version, or from 140lb/in to 135lb/in on the Cortina GT. The result was a car that rode better, but seemed to handle at least as well – though today's critics should recall that roadholding standards overall have improved dramatically over the last thirty years.

At the same time, and because of the increased clearances in the front wheel boxes, the steering geometry had been altered so that the Mark II could be turned much more sharply than had been possible in the Mark I.

Driveline – little change, yet

For the first model year, it seemed that the only important engine improvement over the last of the Mark Is was a 53.3bhp/1297cc 'Base' engine instead of the earlier car's 48.5bhp/1198cc unit. This

change was very simply provided by a short-stroke version of the 1500 using a shallower cylinder block, as valve sizes, camshaft and bearings were all the same as before.

This engine and the Mark II's 1500 engine (but not the GT) were the first to use a new Ford-designed carburettor called the GPD. Ford admitted that it was 'very similar' to the Solex units previously employed, but when questioners suggested the word 'copy' there was never a response ...

For export only – and then only for a limited number of markets – the earlier 1198cc engine was retained, but this was never available in cars sold in the UK.

There were no major transmission changes, except that Borg Warner automatic transmission became available with the 1.3-litre engine. Even that innovation was a big mistake – the 1.3-litre engine wasn't really powerful enough to cope with a 1960s generation automatic, and its torque converter allowed power losses. (That option would be dropped for future Cortinas.)

For manual transmission cars, the good news was that a diaphragm spring clutch had been standardised, while the remote gearbox linkage for the GT model had been improved: this was done

by providing a different rear casing with the lever sprouting directly from it.

Even so, there was still no change to the gearbox ratios at first. As ever, there was a yawning gap between second and third ratios: as with the Mk I cars, this was just about acceptable on the less sporty models but was a severe irritant for GT buyers. By this time, in fact, Ford couldn't plead that it had no alternative as a revised set of ratios had already been developed to fit in the same gearbox casing. These were first seen in the V4-engined Corsairs introduced in 1965, and were almost immediately adopted for the last model year of the Lotus-Cortina Mk I. They had been found to be much more satisfactory.

The comparison between the new and original internal ratios is shown in the table.

Although this made second gear much more usable in modern traffic, Ford's product planners were still stubborn, and would not adopt the new ratios at first. Spokesmen would mutter about hill-climbing capabilities when heavily laden, unit costs ... in fact anything that would divert a casual query.

Resistance in the face of determined customer nagging, however, was futile, and the change had to be made. From January 1967 – only three months after launch of the Mark II – the GT model was given the revised ratios. Not only was this transmission much better

As with the earlier type, the Cortina GT Mark II was available in two-door and four-door forms. In those days, please note, cross-ply tyres were still standard equipment.

The Mk II estate car had a smoother, more anonymous style than the Mark I, and went on to sell very strongly.

suited to the GT engine, it also made Ford-Motorsport's 'uprated second gear' kit obsolete overnight!

When the Mark II went on sale in October 1966, the combination of two-door and four-door, 1.3 and 1.5-litre, and various equipment packs meant that there were already eight models in the range, even though the estate car and Lotus-Cortina varieties were yet to come. (See table for price examples.)

For the next two years, Ford carried on adding to the range, improving the specifications and – as usual – trying to make sure that there was a Cortina for everybody. The Cortina GT's revised gear ratios came first – but that improvement would not be made on any other Mark IIs.

Then came the launch of the estate car derivative, an introduction which needed to be delayed until February 1967, simply to allow the hard-pressed Dagenham production facilities fit in the latest changes to its press shop and body assembly departments!

An estate car rear end suited this style, and Ford was boastful of the 70cu.ft stowage space on offer. Mechanically, the estates were almost the same as the saloons, except that automatic transmission was not available with the 1.3-litre engine and rear-axle movement was controlled by lever arm instead of telescopic dampers, this last

As with the Mark I car, the rear seat was arranged to give the maximum possible 'floor' support when folded flat, the forward section of the seat cushion somersaulting through 180 degrees to make this possible.

'Kent' engine for 1968

Only a year after introducing the Mk II, Ford launched a much revised car, complete with the improved cross-flow range of 'Kent' engines. More powerful and more efficient than before with, for the first time, a 1.6-litre version, too, they gave the Cortina a massive boost.

This was also the point at which Ford-UK cars first bowed to new USA exhaust emission regulations; for this market belt-driven air pumps (to inject into the exhaust manifold) were standardised.

Although the new engine made all Ford's technical headlines at

| Original: | Top 1.00 | 3rd 1.412 | 2nd 2.40 | 1st 3.54 | Rev 3.96:1 |
| Revised: | Top 1.00 | 3rd 1.397 | 2nd 2.01 | 1st 2.972 | Rev 3.324:1 |

1300 de Luxe (2-door)	£669
1500 Super (4-door)	£755
1500GT (2-door)	£810
1500GT (4-door)	£835

change being made to reduce body mounting intrusion into the estate loading space. One consequence of the redesigned rear end was that a smaller petrol tank of only 8 gallons/36 litres was specified.

Kent engine – a new Ford building-block

From 1967 when it was introduced, to 1983 when the last series-production units were built at Dagenham, the four-cylinder 'Kent' engine was the most important building-block in Ford-of-Europe's line-up. Like the earlier four-cylinder unit it replaced, each and every engine had an 80.96mm cylinder bore. By using different cylinder block heights, long or short strokes and crankshafts to suit, millions were manufactured in 1.1, 1.3 and 1.6-litre sizes.

Years after the machinery at Dagenham had been re-worked to allow 1.6-litre (later 1.8-litre) overhead-camshaft diesel engines to be produced, Kent engines were still being made, or re-manufactured, on other sites in the UK and overseas.

The Kent engine was developed as an all-can-do package for introduction in the late 1960s, and it would be used in many different Fiesta, Escort, Cortina and Capri models. It was also supplied to a variety of specialist manufacturers, such as Morgan, TVR, Lotus and Marcos.

Although the 1.6-litre version had the longest stroke of all such Kent engines – 77.62mm – its rock-solid, five-bearing bottom end also served as the basis for the famous race-winning Ford Cosworth BDA engines – the largest of which were eventually pushed out to 2.0 litres.

The Kent was not an all-new engine for the basic cylinder blocks, machining dimensions, bore centres and crankshaft layout – the bare bones, as it were – were those of the earlier Anglia 105E, Cortina, Classic, Corsair four-cylinder engine. All the novelties were in the cylinder head and the breathing arrangements.

The principal novelties were that the Kent used a cross-flow cylinder head – with the carburettor, ports and inlet manifold on the right side of the engine and the exhaust ports and manifold on the left-side – and that the combustion chamber was formed almost entirely in the top of the pistons. There was, effectively, a bowl in the top of the pistons, which explains why Ford engineers originally knew it as the BIP engine (bowl-in-piston). There was no combustion space at all in the 1.3-litre cylinder head (which had a totally flat machined face) and only a small recess in that of the 1.6-litre unit.

The specification was updated in the early 1970s, and a whole variety of different carburettors and manifolds were used in different models over the years, but otherwise the Kent of the early 1980s was very similar indeed to the Kent of 1967.

Not only was the Kent a free-revving and virtually unburstable unit in standard form, it was also very tuneable. Not for nothing was it chosen as the basis of the Formula Ford single-seater racing formula, which was taken up as a 'starter formula' all around the world.

In road use, experience showed that as long as the oil was regularly changed, it was possible go on driving otherwise sadly neglected cars for a great many years. Parts, if not complete engines, are still readily available today.

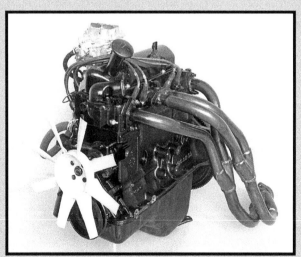

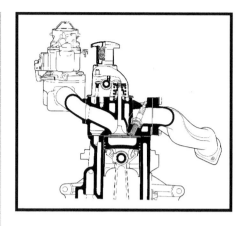

The famous bowl-in-piston engine also featured a cross-flow cylinder head. The combustion chamber of these engines was formed entirely in the top of the piston.

the end of 1967, it was yet another new Cortina derivative – the 1600E – which got all the marketing attention. Here was a classic case of Ford seeing a gap in the market, and going boldly to fill it. With very little investment – and virtually no development – required, Ford got itself a new model which was not only a commercial success but one that became a real icon.

'It was a marketing-inspired programme,' Harry Calton remembers, 'with virtually no investment. It had a very nice interior, plus all that wood. It also had those nice Rostyle wheels – the ones that rusted very quickly!'

The theme was put together by Howard Panton at very short notice – really only a week or two – in 1967, and was all based on the new cross-flow GT package. The 'E' stood for Executive. Was it really Walter Hayes, however, who sparked off this project?

The legendary bowl-in-piston 'Kent' engine was standardised in the Cortina Mark II range from the autumn of 1967. This was the GT derivative, complete with downdraught two-choke Weber carburettor.

Engine	Original 1966-67 models	From Sept 1967 (for '68 model year)
1298cc	53.5bhp/5000rpm	58bhp/5000rpm
1498cc	61bhp/4700rpm	
1498cc GT	78bhp/5200rpm	
1598cc		71bhp/5000rpm
1598cc GT		88bhp/5200rpm

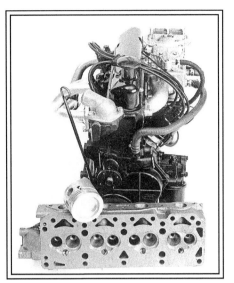

Cylinder head and piston detail of the new-generation 'Kent' engine.

'I once spent £400 out of Public Affairs budgets,' Hayes comments, 'to have Hoopers do a leather and wood interior on the Mk II Cortina ... and that eventually became the 1600E.'

Yet Harry Calton states quite firmly that Hayes was against the 1600E at first, saying that it was debasing the Cortina GT and the Lotus-Cortina, but that he came to support it afterwards!

In any case Ford's first 'E' car – the Mk IV Zodiac Executive – arrived at the London Motor Show of October 1966, establishing the wooden fascia, plush seating, thick carpets, and top-of-the-range equipment combination which later cars would follow. The Corsair 2000E followed it in January 1967, so the Cortina 1600E was third in a line which would eventually stretch to Capris and Escorts!

Structurally and mechanically, the 1600E was pure Cortina GT, originally with the lowered and stiffened Lotus-Cortina Mk II suspension settings complete with radius arms, and 5.5in Rostyle road wheels. Later versions would use modified suspension settings, but the basic character of the car never changed in three years.

In transatlantic marketing terms, the 'Unique Selling Proposition' was to be found in the

The Cortina 1600E announced at the end of 1967 was the best-equipped Cortina yet seen, and was sold with Rostyle wheels and lowered suspension as standard.

The 1600E's trim and furnishing set new standards for the Cortina. (The rear seating was arranged purely for two occupants.)

The 1600E, 1967-70, could be identified from any angle, but especially from the rear, where the combination of Rostyle wheels, badging and a motif on the rear quarters was unmistakeable.

The 1600E used the same basic instrument panel as that of the Cortina GT and Lotus-Cortina types, but this was clad with a wood panel, as were the door cappings. Note the plushy seat styles, and the aluminium-spoked steering wheel.

interior, where there was a wood-panelled fascia and door cappings, an aluminium spoked steering wheel, extra sound deadening, special high-grade carpets, trim and seats – the fronts having reclining mechanisms. Externally, there were special colours (one of them widely nicknamed 'Purple People Eater,' from a current popular song), extra driving lamps and an optional vinyl roof covering.

At first the 1600E was only available as a four-door saloon, but for some export markets a two-door saloon was added from the beginning of 1969. An estate car version was never available. The 1600E was a remarkable success, paying back its investment many times, for in those three years totals of 55,833 four-door and 2749 two-door saloons were sold.

This, of course, was only one of the improvements Ford made to the Cortina Mk II at all levels and for all markets. From mid-1968 the earlier 'export-only' Mk II 1200 was replaced by a new cross-flow 1098cc-engined Cortina. The radius arms, which had once located the rear axle of GTs, were dropped from home market cars (and those going to many export territories) at the beginning of 1968, to improve what Ford called the NVH (Noise-Vibration-Harshness)

Although the 1600E two-door model was not available in the UK, it was sold in several export markets.

characteristics; radius arms were always retained on the 1600E.

At the same time, Cortina Supers inherited the GT-style remote control gearchange, the GT got radial-ply tyres as standard, and fully reclining front seats also became optional on the De Luxe, which acquired carpets instead of floor mats.

This was also the season in which a desirable (but rare) version – the Cortina GT Estate – became available from the Special Vehicle Order department. This wasn't quite the same, mechanically, as the saloons – the rear axle was controlled by lever arm dampers – but it was still a very brisk 95mph machine, which now has a 'classic' following.

The expected mid-life facelift arrived in October 1968 for all Cortinas, involving trim, equipment *and* mechanical improvements. On the outside there was a new grille, while in the cabin there were fascia modifications (especially to the GT, 1600E and Lotus-Cortina types), a new centre console and (at last!) a home for the handbrake on the tunnel, instead of under the fascia in an awful 'umbrella handle' arrangement. There was also a new internal bonnet-release

mechanism, and a fully fused electrical system.

New-style front seats in deep-embossed PVC were specified to Super, GT, 1600E and Lotus types, while fully reclining seats were available as extras on two-door cars for the first time.

Technically the most important innovation was the introduction of a new gearbox casing and selector mechanism, complete with what is known as a 'single rail remote-control' selector mechanism. This was done for several reasons – the most important being that costs were reduced and the assembly was more compact.

In October 1968, therefore, the Cortina's Mk II retail prices were as per the table below.

For 1969 the fourteen-strong Cortina Mk II range held sway, always up at the top of British sales charts, selling strongly overseas, built from kits in far-flung countries – and making far more money for Ford than its sponsors could ever have hoped.

No amount of company changes or new faces could harm this phenomenal machine. Ford-Europe was happy to hold up the Cortina as an example to Ford-Germany (where the latest Taunus was not selling at all well). Meanwhile, Bill Batty took over smoothly as Managing Director in the UK, from Allan Barke, Terry Beckett was about to become Ford-Europe's Vice-President of European Sales Operations, and Sam Toy took over from him in the UK.

The Cortina sold so well, so consistently, that British management had total confidence in it:

'We were convinced that we needed to change it every four years, 'Terry Beckett stated,' but as to

1969 Model_		Retail Price
1300	2-door De Luxe	£792
	4-door De Luxe	£818
	Estate De Luxe	£914
1600	2-door De Luxe	£837
	4-door De Luxe	£863
	Estate De Luxe	£958
1600	2-door Super	£856
	4-door Super	£882
	Estate Super	£978
- automatic transmission for above cars		£87
GT	2-door	£939
	4-door	£965
	Estate	£1076
1600E	4-door	£1073
Lotus-Cortina		£1163

From the autumn of 1968, Ford began marketing a special version of the Cortina – the Cortina GT Estate – the fastest load carrier so far in this range.

where it would lead us, we didn't really have to determine.'

The final months

Not long before the Mk II range and the 1600E were finally discontinued, Ford pulled a typical marketing coup. Taking advantage of the nationwide interest in the 1970 football World Cup – and the fact that England was reigning World Champion – Ford pitched in with some high-profile sponsorship.

In the spring of 1970 a fleet of identical Cortina 1600Es was produced, given a series of Essex 'GWC' registrations, and each member of the England squad got the use of a car that year. It was good PR, but it wasn't totally successful on the football front, as England didn't make it to the final. [Not that Ford was too disappointed. Just before the tournament began there was an equally high-profile trans-continental rally, where a 'works' entry of seven Escorts in the *Daily Mirror* World Cup Rally (London to Mexico) dominated the event – the cars finishing 1st, 3rd, 5th, 6th and 8th!]

Sam Toy, that extrovert salesman who went on to become Ford-UK's Chairman in the late 1970s, sums up this type of Cortina perfectly:

'Somehow the Cortina became the great love of everyone at Ford Motor Co., and of the dealers, too. It was wonderful cash flow for them. I'm not sure it could ever be done again – it would need the same combination of good fortune, design, marketing – and coincidence.

'I can remember that when we went from the Mark II to the Mark III, the Mark II was really ringing the penetration bells, and when we had the dealers' meeting to launch the Mark III, the Mark II was absolutely at the zenith of its market share.

'The dealers couldn't understand why on earth we were changing it. I said: "Give it another year, and it wouldn't be as successful – and getting back up is a darned sight harder than staying up there!"

This, of course, was in the autumn of 1970, when the Cortina Mark II was finally discontinued. No-one could have known what traumas would follow in 1971!

For export only...

In the late 1960s, Ford also developed a 1.1-litre version of the Mark II, but only for sale in markets where the vehicle taxation regime made it saleable. By most British standards, this was a Cortina with marginal performance, because its 1098cc power unit only produced 49.5bhp at 5500rpm, and 59lb/ft of torque at 3000rpm. It was,

Cortina Savage – V6 performance by Jeff Uren

When the original Ford Cortina Savage appeared in 1967, it was a private venture, little more than a 128bhp 3-litre 'Essex' V6 engine transplant in a Cortina Mk II shell. Conceived by forty-year-old Jeff Uren, it was built by his Race Proved business in West London. At first the Savage was underdeveloped, it could overheat, and it didn't handle very well – but it had the sort of easy, laid-back, no-problem performance that no production-line Cortina could offer, so it sold very well indeed. For the next few years it gained Ford's acceptance, but not its full-blown approval.

Racer, fixer, team manager

If you knew some of Jeff Uren's background, you could see why this should be so, for by that time he had already done great things with Fords in motorsport. His first link with the marque came in 1955, when he started rallying in a side-valve Ford Anglia 100E, and soon afterwards raced in a Willment-converted Prefect. Then, in 1958, he started racing as a private owner in a Ford Zephyr Mk II, and a year later won the BRSCC Saloon Car Championship in the same car.

From 1960 to 1962 he ran Ford-UK's motorsport efforts, organised the Ford-USA Falcon programme for the 1963 Monte Carlo rally, and then got involved with Ford dealer John Willment's team. This relationship led him not only to race a 7-litre Galaxie, but to prepare a team of Cortina GTs to take part in the BRSCC Saloon Car Championship of 1963 (see Chapter 4).

For the next four years he worked in harness with the Willment organisation, but after John Willment moved on to found JW Automotive Engineering – and to run the famous Ford GT40 race car team which John Wyer managed so impressively – Jeff struck out on his own.

V6 engine, Cortina shell

Jeff Uren set up Race Proved Ltd, operating from a workshop at Hanwell in London W7, where his small team rapidly built up the first '3-litre Cortina

Mk II,' electing to call it a Cortina 'Savage.' In later years Jeff admitted that there were all manner of problems with the early cars, notably because the engines tended to overheat until a revised cooling system could be worked out, and because the big V6 engine was so heavy that the weight distribution caused severe handling problems.

By 1967, however, the design had settled down enough for sales to begin, and Uren was delighted to get tacit approval of his conversion from Ford:

'Walter Hayes wangled quite a lot of 1600E Cortinas for us to convert,' Uren later commented, 'although they were very scarce at the time. He approved of the Savage because it put Fords into the hands of a different class of user – older people, quite well-off, who bought them as fun cars.'

There was nothing unique about the idea of shoe-horning a V6 'Essex' engine into a Cortina or a Corsair shell – Crayford, the convertible specialist from Kent, tried it even earlier – but it was not easy to get it right and to make the conversion feel like a factory-developed machine. Uren, notoriously prickly and a stickler for 'getting it right,' made sure that his Savage was as good as it could be.

It was not, however, to the Ford engineers' liking, as one insider reminded me:

'Whenever he came and talked to our engineers, they would say: "Yes, it's a nice conversion, the engine doesn't overheat, but what are you doing about the back axle, and what are you doing about the gearbox?" Jeff always pretended to be a lot closer to the factory than he actually was ... but if you bought a Uren-converted Cortina it retained the Ford warranty on paint and trim, but it never applied to anything else.'

A bit of good publicity, at the right time, usually helps. *Autocar* tested an early Savage in August 1967, when it discovered that XJH 234F could reach 104mph, sprint from rest to 60mph in 8.8 seconds, and reach the quarter-mile marker in a mere 16.6 seconds. By any standards, this made it a seriously quick Cortina – faster than the recently launched

Lotus-Cortina Mk II and with a more flexible engine – all at 18.9mpg.

This particular car (based on a pre-cross-flow 1500GT, rather than the 1600E which followed) was priced at £1365 and was, by any standards, a very comprehensive conversion. The body shell needed a lot of re-work in and around the engine bay, and there was also a modified cross-member to clear the different sump of the V6 engine.

Apart from the larger radiator, a

Jeff Uren's Cortina Savage was a sophisticated engine-transplant model, using a 3-litre V6 Zodiac-type engine in the Cortina shell. (Fast? You bet!)

Powr-Lok limited slip differential, and 5.5in (Lotus-type) road wheels with Goodyear radial ply tyres, the Savage also had different spring rates, roll-bar and damper settings and modified front camber angles.

There was an extra eight-gallon fuel tank mounted in the front of the boot (above the line of the rear axle).

As *Autocar* wrote at the time:

'The result is about as near to an American car as one can get in Britain – a light body backed up with a great deal of power and torque from a relatively lazy engine ...

'Although the car is so docile and well-behaved in town, it really does hitch up its skirts and get moving on the open road, in a manner that will leave practically everything else standing. The standard Lotus final drive ratio of 3.78:1 is rather too low ...

'This sort of drag take-off is motoring

indeed, and not until one gets into the realms of the 4.7-litre Ford Mustang, 7-litre Olds Tornado or Jaguar 420 can one really start to make comparisons ...

'It is not often that the test staff are so unanimous in their praise for a car. To us the Savage seems the ideal form of modern transport ...'

This sort of road test was just what Race Proved needed to get Ford's long-term approval, and the company certainly capitalised on it.

In the next few years, Savage conversions were not only carried out on Cortina saloons, but also on estate cars, and the same basic transplant operation was later carried out (but in smaller numbers) on Cortina Mk III, Mk IV and Mk V types.

In the Mk III structure, for instance, Race Proved could install a Tecalemit fuel-injected 3-litre V6 engine for which no less than 218bhp was claimed. In that form, and as tested in *Motor*, the Mk III GXL had a top speed of 131mph, 0-60mph in 7.4 seconds, 0-100mph in 20.7 seconds – and a towering fuel thirst of 11.6mpg! Later, too, the same sort of conversion was offered in the 2000E shell, which made for a particularly luxurious package.

It was what *Motor* called the 'absolute ultimate in hot Cortinas,' costing £205 for the engine conversion, £104 for a special exhaust system and an extra £25 for fitting.

All in all, about 1700 such cars were built, though all but sixty of them seem to have been built on the Mk II platform. At peak in 1968 and 1969, fifteen or even twenty cars were being completed every week, all of them from complete new cars. Somewhere, somehow, a lot of barely used 1600GT 'Kent' engines had to be sold off.

The specification, too, changed gradually. Early cars used Lotus/Corsair 2000E types of four-speed gearboxes, and I notice from a 1968-69 specification that overdrive was also made available, as was optional automatic transmission, though I don't know how many of those types were ever built.

England's World Cup football team was supplied with a fleet of white Cortina 1600Es in the spring of 1970. The cars which have survived in the 'GWC ... H' sequence are now keenly sought by Cortina enthusiasts.

in fact, a slightly more powerful version of the engine currently being fitted to many thousands of the new Escort models, and naturally had to be linked to the 4.44:1 final drive ratio.

To get a feel for marginal Cortina motoring, *Autocar* borrowed a Greek market demonstrator for test, finding that this left-hand-drive model also had fittings they had long forgotten, including a steering column gearchange and a bench front seat!

The performance could not be described as exciting for top speed was only 71mph, 0-60mph acceleration took 27.1 seconds,

Go-faster conversions – Mk I and Mk II

In the 1960s there were no stifling British regulations governing exhaust emissions and Type Approval, so the 'go-faster' business was thriving. From time to time, specialists tried their hands at improving the Cortina:

In 1963 Alexander Engineering offered a twin-SU conversion on the original 1200, which included a gas-flowed cylinder head, a 9.2:1 compression ratio, and double valve springs, all for £55. This gave a noticeable, but not startling, improvement in performance – with 0-60mph cut from 22.5 to 18.0 seconds, and top speed raised from 77mph to 84mph – yet the overall fuel consumption increased from 30mpg to around 22mpg.

Later in the year Lawrencetune's conversion for the Cortina GT was more ambitious. For £125, a considerable sum in those days and one sixth the price of the original car itself, there was a fully-modified head, a new camshaft profile, and twin side-draught twin-choke 40DCOE Weber carburettors.

The improvement was startling for the top speed was pushed up from 94mph to no less than 105mph, with 0-60mph acceleration cut from 13.9 seconds to 10.2 seconds. Fuel efficiency held up remarkably well, at about 25mpg overall, quite a surprise considering the legendary thirst of such Weber carburettors.

In effect, this meant that, for a total of £874, the Lawrencetune GT offered similar performance to the recently announced Lotus-Cortina, with little of the temperament and none of the chassis unreliability. This, in many ways, was the specification adopted by the 'works' Cortina GT rally cars in 1964 and 1965, before the team turned to Lotus-Cortinas.

The Willment 'Super Sprint' Cortina GT of 1965, in which racing team manager Jeff Uren had been involved, was even more extreme, with more performance (108bhp instead of 78bhp), ferocious fuel consumption (down to 13mpg at times) and a colossal conversion cost of £559, which made the car much more expensive than the Lotus-Cortina.

For this the Willment buyer (there could not have been many of them!) received a complete engine conversion – head, camshaft, internals, and twin Weber 40 DCOEs, along with the uprated second-gear transmission, lowered and stiffened suspension, wide-rim wheels, modified brakes, Cox GT3 front seats ... in other words, a no-holds-barred rebuild.

There was even more performance than with the Lawrencetune kit – with a top speed of 111mph, though 0-60mph in 10.9 seconds was very similar. A measure of the overall improvement was that the car accelerated nearly twice as fast to 90mph as the standard car, though still not quite as fast as the unmodified Lotus-Cortina.

There was also a less-extreme version, the Willment Sprint GT, for which 'only' 92bhp was claimed, this being achieved by work on the cylinder head manifolds, but only by re-jetting the carburettor – the result being a £54 engine conversion (plus £27 for fitting) which gave a 104mph top speed, 0-60mph in 9.5 seconds, and even 0-100mph in 45.6 seconds.

When certain suspension and brake modifications were added in, a total transformation cost £165 on a new car prepared by Willment, or £222 as a complete conversion kit of pieces. By any standards I rate this as good value – and so did the customers.

IWR (owned by successful racing driver Ian Walker) clearly thought the Willment package was excessive, offering a much more modest engine conversion for £125. Superficially this looked standard – the downdraught Weber carburettor and the Ford tubular exhaust manifold were retained – but with changes including a reworked cylinder head, a 10.5:1 compression ratio, and an IWR camshaft profile. Peak power at the rear wheels rose from 55bhp to a claimed 80bhp.

Even so, the performance improvement was modest, with top speed rising only to 96mph, and 0-60mph dropped from 13.9 seconds to 11.8 seconds. In fairness, this *Autocar* test was carried out with a low rear axle ratio (4.44:1), so the car was over-revving in

top gear at maximum speed.

On a more modest scale, Taurus asked only £39 (£62.50 with fitting and testing) for a conversion of the Cortina GT engine which involved no more than a modified cylinder head and a different camshaft. The top speed was 101mph – 7mph higher than standard – with 0-60mph in just 11.0 seconds, which sounded like a real bargain. I have never driven one of these particular cars – have any survived?

SuperSpeed of Ilford, Essex marketed a very similar type of conversion – internal engine changes but the same carburettor, plus work on the suspension, for which a total of £120 was asked. SuperSpeed reckoned it had pushed the power up to 90bhp, and the top speed was no less than 103mph.

Chris Steele Engineering was probably the first to offer a good tune-up conversion for the new cross-flow 'Kent' engine. This was appropriate, as the same firm was already adept at producing fine 'blueprinted' engines for Formula Ford cars.

This was rather a specialised conversion, as the steep price of £295 (or only £150 if done on a new car) confirms. Superficially and visually there were no changes, for the engine was subject only to a meticulous Formula Ford-type 'blueprinting' process.

The cylinder head was also gas-flowed, the ports polished, and the combustion chambers were reshaped, but because the camshaft was also reprofiled, the claim that a Steele engine produced 116bhp with an F exhaust system was at least believable.

Autosport reported that a Cortina 1600GT, thus modified, had a top speed of 104mph, with 0-60mph acceleration in 10.5 seconds, and that:

'... here is a race-developed engine that really works in a road car, and there seems sure to be a steady demand for their road engine.'

This was not true, in fact, for the conversion price was really too high: the cost of a Steele 1600GT Cortina GT was very similar to a standard, and very desirable, Lotus-Cortina Mk II.

The Cortina was named 'Car of the Year' at the end of 1964. Ford celebrated by taking cars, and racing drivers, to Cortina in Italy where, among other celebrations, a Cortina was driven down the ski run!

yet overall fuel consumption was a miserable 22.3mpg overall. By any standards, this was the slowest-ever Cortina. [That was with 49.5bhp. As I write these words, my current personal car has nearly 200bhp, weighs nearly 3000lb/26.5cwt, yet returns better than 30mpg in everyday use. Automotive engineering has certainly advanced a lot in the last thirty years!]

As the test concluded:

'Because of the low gearing and the need to rev the engine hard almost all the time, the 1100 Cortina is not a relaxing car to drive, and one needs to concentrate hard on the road ahead in order to keep up what speed there is ... Here at home we hope earnestly that no misguided government ever decides to put a tax on engine size ...'

3

LOTUS-CORTINA TWIN-CAM PERFORMANCE

Lotus-Cortina! It was the most glamorous of all these cars, but it remained controversial throughout its life. Designed to win races for Ford-UK, and successful in that, it was nevertheless a slow seller. Enthusiasts loved it, some owners hated it, Ford dealers suspected it, and Ford's accountants must have wished it had never been invented.

But the Lotus-Cortina did its job. No sooner did the twin-cam-engined car reach the race tracks than the victories started rolling in. It was fast, spectacular, and a great talking-point, so Ford bosses could forgive its obvious failings. As a commercial proposition, however, it was a disaster.

I don't suppose we will ever know how close Ford came to ditching the Lotus-Cortina project in 1964. This model, now legendary and an object of desire for all classic Ford enthusiasts, was unreliable at first, built to appallingly low standards, and took ages to get into the showrooms. Once there, it often remained for months, as insurance companies didn't understand it and neither did the Ford salesmen who were meant to move the metal.

Even as the 'classic car' movement built up in the 1970s, Lotus-Cortinas still got a bad press. Go-faster merchants tended to look at Escort Twin-Cams, see that they were smaller and lighter, and choose them instead. Now the tide has turned. Lotus-Cortinas – particularly Mk Is – are extremely desirable machines.

It is important that these cars should be preserved, understood and loved, for when the very first model was unveiled in 1963, it was the very first 'fast Ford' of them all. Everyone out there who owns a hot Escort, Capri, Fiesta or whatever, should know that Ford's sporting heritage was born at Cheshunt in the early 1960s.

Hayes + Chapman = dynamite

If the car had been cancelled in the mid-1960s, no-one at Ford would have wanted to be associated with it, but because it became famous, any number of people like to give their version of its origins.

Today's popular legend is that the Lotus-Cortina story really started in 1962, when Walter Hayes arrived at Ford to take over the Public Affairs department. This job included overseeing Ford's activities in motorsport, and it wasn't long before Hayes got the go ahead to start planning a race-winning saloon.

However, this may be an oversimplification. As Hamish Orr-Ewing commented:

'This is a bitty story. Pat Hennessy always had a liking for Colin Chapman. Cheeky Colin would have had no hesitation – he would ring up Hennessy and he would get through, whereas no-one else in the world would get past the secretary.

Henry Taylor, who led Ford's rally team in the mid-1960s, not only drove the 'works' Lotus-Cortinas in motorsport, but was also an invaluable link between Colin Chapman and Ford management.

Colin Chapman – genius, fast talker, ruthless entrepreneur – founded Lotus in the 1950s, and persuaded Ford that Lotus should build the Lotus-Cortina (from 1963 to 1966).

Colin Chapman (in sunglasses) Walter Hayes (on his left) and Ford Competition Manager Alan Platt (back to camera, document in hands) talking tactics at Boreham in the 1960s.

'He worked on Hennessy to be allowed to do something on the Cortina. That resulted in a fair wind being given to us to discuss with Colin Chapman the various possibilities. Phil Ives and I, we always played a peripheral role in this, because Hennessy was ever-present, and Colin Chapman had a direct line through.'

The Beckett version is slightly different: 'Pat Hennessy and I then got Colin Chapman to give us a souped-up version – a Lotus-Cortina – this was to spread a bit of stardust on the programme. We were under no illusions, and it took Colin about another twelve months before he was in production.'

Walter Hayes, in fact, probably gave the 'why don't we ...?' programme the impetus it needed. As a national newspaper editor, he had been using Colin Chapman to write a motor sporting column well before this project matured. He kept his contacts when he joined Ford, and encouraged Chapman all the way when he and Harry Mundy developed the twin-cam engine.

To summarise, Harry Calton's memory tells us a lot:

'I think Walter reacted to some extent to Chapman's nagging, that we *had* to do something to lift the Cortina, to brighten it up.'

There is also the long-running 'BMC factor' to consider for, as *The Autocar* wrote in its description of the Lotus-Cortina in January 1963:

'It is also not unreasonable to imagine that Sir Patrick Hennessy and his managerial colleagues at Dagenham became envious of the success of the Mini-Cooper in competition and mindful of the resulting publicity.'

If the origins of the car were rather muddy, the strategy was razor-sharp. Ford and Colin Chapman of Lotus got together and worked out a brilliant scheme for the making of a new 'homologation special' – really the first such car in Britain, for the contemporary BMC Mini-Cooper S did not involve a new power plant. Lotus (with the help of Keith Duckworth at Cosworth) was already developing

Walter Hayes of Ford (left) and Colin Chapman of Lotus were two of the most important personalities behind the Ford/Lotus liaison of the 1960s and 1970s.

The Lotus-Ford twin-cam engine was originally designed for Lotus to use in sportscars, then adopted for the Ford Lotus-Cortina and, later, the Escort Twin-Cam. Below the cylinder head face, this engine was based on the standard 1.5-litre Cortina unit.

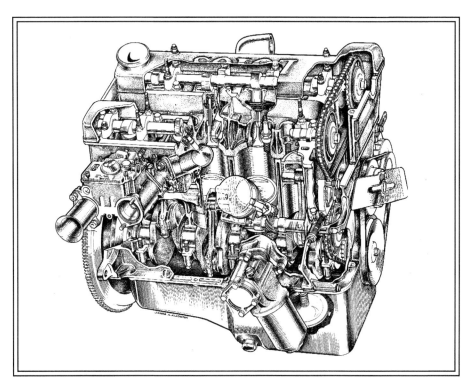

a new twin-cam engine based on a Ford pushrod engine, while Ford was about to reveal the ultra-light Cortina, of which a Cortina GT was planned. Much of the Cortina GT's chassis, including the brakes and other details, could be used, thus reducing development time to a minimum.

Twin-cam cylinder head, Cortina bottom end

The project centred on the development of a brand-new four-cylinder Lotus twin-cam engine, which was to be based on the bottom end of the existing Anglia/Classic/Cortina unit. At the time of its birth, Lotus did not have designers who could do that job, nor the ability to manufacture engines of its own – but to Colin Chapman the visionary these were trifling problems which could be solved simply by buying in expertise.

Chapman's first bright idea was for a new engine that would be at least as powerful as the Coventry-Climax single-cam units of a type which were already being used in the Lotus Elite road cars, and various Lotus racing sports cars, but which would be a lot cheaper. The new engine, he thought, could take over from the Coventry-Climax unit, and could also power a new range of Lotus road cars – which became the Elan and Elan Plus Two – that he wanted to produce in the next few years.

The intention was to use the

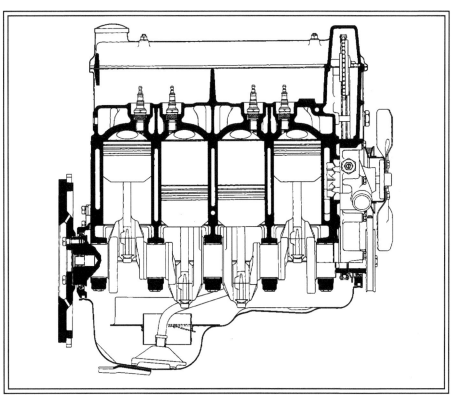

The Cortina's rugged five-main-bearing bottom end was an ideal base for the Lotus twin-cam conversion. The cylinder head had a classic 1950s-racing-vintage, part-spherical combustion chamber layout.

The Lotus-Cortina inlet manifold stubs were cast integrally with the cylinder head.

little-modified bottom end of an existing mass-production engine (it did not necessarily have to be a Ford at this stage) – one which would therefore be simple to repair and maintain – but to use an entirely new eight-valve twin-cam aluminium cylinder head. By using the latest F1 knowledge of top-end breathing, combustion and camshaft design, the specific output was to be a huge increase over the push-rod head it would replace.

It did not take Chapman long to choose a Ford for his donor engine, mainly because his successful Formula Junior single-seaters (with Jim Clark as star driver) were already powered by Cosworth-prepared and much-modified Ford Anglia 105E power units.

At that time, as far as I can see, Lotus had no intention of supplying engines to any other customers at first, especially Ford who had absolutely no use for them. Although the Anglia/Classic engine still only officially existed in three-bearing, 997cc (105E) and 1340cc (109E) form in 1961, Chapman already knew – through the industry's grapevine and his racing connections – that a five-bearing, 1498cc unit (116E) was on the way.

One of Chapman's best friends was Harry Mundy, who had acquired a glittering reputation as a race-engine designer. Although currently technical editor of *The Autocar*, he was always in close touch with engine design trends.

Having worked with Alvis and ERA in the 1930s, and the complex V16 BRM Grand Prix engine of the 1940s, Mundy had then joined Coventry-Climax to design famous racing engines such as the FWA/FWE (used in the Lotus Elite) and the FPF twin-cam which powered so many famous F1 and F2 racing cars of the period.

During the winter of 1960-61, as a freelance project Mundy had already designed a new twin-cam cylinder head for the French Facel Vega Facellia, but this project foundered when the company ran short of money. When Chapman heard of this, he approached Mundy, commissioning him to do the same for Lotus.

Early in 1961, therefore, Mundy laid out a new twin-cam cylinder head to sit on the Anglia/Cortina block. Like all the best race engines of the day, this had inverted tappets between the camshaft lobes and the valve stems themselves, part-spherical cylinder heads, valves opposed at 54 degrees, and was fuelled by twin side-draught, dual-choke Weber carburettors. [The days of narrow valve angles and four valves per cylinder, not to mention fuel injection, were still some years into the future ...]

To keep down the costs, and the required financial investment, the entire 116E bottom end – cylinder block, pistons, connecting rods, crankshaft, distributor and other details – were all retained. Later, for series production, a different crankshaft casting would be specified, along with slightly different pistons. Even the pushrod engine's original camshaft in the side of the cylinder block was also retained, though in this application it was only used as a shaft to continue driving the electrical distributor and the oil pump.

Camshaft drive was to be by chain from the front of the crankshaft, and in production-standard units the inlet manifolds were cast into the main cylinder head casting.

Harry once told me that his fee for this design job was a choice between £200 (perhaps equivalent to two or three weeks' worth of his considerable salary at the time) or a £1 royalty on every engine subsequently built: 'I made the wrong choice,' he admitted. 'I took the flat fee, but when Lotus announced the building of the 25,000th engine some years later, I met Chapman at the reception and suggested I should change my mind. Colin, being Colin, just grinned and told me to bugger off!'

Harry Mundy's scheme was then detailed by Richard Ansdale (who was also responsible, in detail, for the entire chain-driven front end of the engine). The very first prototype engine was built up on a three-bearing 1340cc bottom end in October 1961 and produced around 85bhp, though this was later improved to 97bhp. Later development engines were built as 1.0-litre, 1.1-litre and three-bearing 1.5-litre units, before the very first five-bearing 1498cc (116E-based) engine ran in May 1962.

This five-bearing engine powered Jim Clark's Lotus 23 racing sportscar in the Nürburgring 1000km race. Clark led for some distance until an exhaust pipe fractured and the car spun off the road. All development was concentrated on this 1.5-litre engine after that.

Yet it was still by no means ready for production. Keith Duckworth, the founder and designing genius behind Cosworth Engineering, was therefore consulted:

'Colin approached us,' Keith says, 'not only to make a racing version of the engine, but to sort it out to go into a production car. It wasn't all bad, but at the time the head joint wasn't sound, the head structure wasn't any good, and its ports didn't look like ports ought to look …

'I didn't think the ports were as free-flowing or as straight as they should be. By that time we did think we had a fair idea of how you should get air, at high velocity, through ports, and to work properly. So we straightened up the ports – we just arbitrarily redesigned them – then we added a bit of structure into the head too.'

Once this work had been done and a solution to the oil breathing arrangements had been found, Duckworth and Chapman agreed that the engine was almost ready to go ahead. Testing of race-prepared engines was so promising – 140bhp was produced without much difficulty – that it seemed silly to build engines a full 102cc under the 1.6-litre class limit.

Accordingly, Lotus arranged that for series production Ford should supply engine bottom ends with the cylinder bores and pistons enlarged from 80.96mm to 82.55mm – which pushed up the swept volume from 1498cc to 1558cc; this was simply achieved by giving the blocks a + 60 thou service overbore. [Incidentally, the Lotus Elan sportscar was introduced in October 1962 with a 1498cc engine, though only

five such cars were ever built before the 1558cc engine came 'on stream,' and those cars were soon re-engined.]

In the nick of time, Lotus arranged for quantities of the complex new cylinder heads to be cast by William Mills (of Wednesbury, Staffs) and for J A Prestwich (of Tottenham, North London, maker of JAP racing motorcycle engines) to machine the heads and assemble complete engines. Engine production, incidentally, would eventually move to JAP's new associate factory, Villers, of Wolverhampton, but before Lotus-Cortina (and Escort Twin-Cam) assembly eventually closed down, Lotus would take engine production 'in house' at its new Hethel factory.

Ford arranged to supply partly built-up bottom ends from Dagenham; JAP completed twin-cam engine assembly and then delivered complete units to Lotus at Cheshunt, in Hertfordshire. Lotus Elans – and later Lotus-Cortinas – were assembled at Cheshunt at this time.

Lotus engine + Cortina structure = Lotus-Cortina

While engine design and development was going ahead, the Hennessy-Hayes-Chapman 'master plan' for the special twin-cam-engined Lotus-Cortina was already taking shape.

The strategy, which never

A-frame to leaf-spring conversion

As I make clear in the main text, Lotus's A-frame suspension layout for the Lotus-Cortina was unreliable, and became very unpopular before it was ditched in favour of Ford's own leaf-spring-plus-radius arms layout.

In 1966 the very enterprising Ian Walker Racing business started selling a conversion which allowed 'A-frame' cars to be converted to the latest specification.

For a mere £50 a 1963-65 car could be updated. Mind you, that was to a straight leaf-spring specification *without* the radius arms which had become part of the latest Lotus-Cortina, and indeed the Cortina GT specifications.

To make up for the lack of radius arms, the IWR conversion used Armstrong Firmaride (adjustable) dampers, and there was also a long, single-piece propeller shaft in the kit.

Clearly this was only halfway to being as effective as the official factory layout for, as Paddy McNally wrote when he tested a converted car in *Autosport*:

'If I were doing the job myself, while I was about it I would fit a substantial Panhard rod to cut out any tendency towards rear-wheel steering, and improve the high-speed stability of the car. The complete conversion, including labour, is priced at £50, which must be considered cheap, if only for your own peace of mind. No longer need you drive with one ear permanently tuned to the hum of the diff ...'

Enthusiasts are not fools, and I suspect that very few of them fell for what was little more than a tuning house's careful rummage through the Ford parts bin. As far as I can judge, this conversion sank with very little trace.

---

varied in the life of the original-shape Lotus-Cortina of 1963-66, was for Lotus to be given a free hand to re-engineer the still-secret Cortina model, basing some of the chassis engineering on what would become the Cortina GT. This was all aimed at producing a car capable of winning the British Saloon Car Championship (which, at this time, was dominated by heavy, 3.8-litre Jaguar Mk 2s) and, if possible, the European series too.

To gain sporting homologation for this new car, 1000 cars would have to be built – or, to put it bluntly, someone at Ford and Lotus would have to assure the RAC MSA that 1000 cars *had* been built. Those were the days in which a gentleman's word was trusted, for no counts or inspections were ever made! This meant that a distribution, marketing and stocking system would have to be set up, and because this car was to be badged as a Ford, that had to be through the Ford dealer network.

Having been rushed ahead of a near-impossible timetable and schedule, the Lotus-Cortina would actually be unveiled in January 1963, though this was some months before deliveries could actually begin. (Incidentally, Ford insisted on calling the car the Cortina-developed-by-Lotus for a long time, before drawing back somewhat and allowing it to be called the Cortina-Lotus.) The first cars, however badly manufactured, would have to be sent out to showrooms, with sporting homologation following behind them, so that the 'works' race cars could start their careers!

Although Ford was anxious to maintain its own rigorous engineering standards, the sheer urgency of the programme had an obvious effect. Sir Patrick Hennessy realised that allowances had to be made for this highly tuned car. In retrospect, this was very wise, for Lotus was not then known for developing very reliable products! For Lotus, incidentally, this car was always the Type 28, while the Ford internal definition was the Type 125E Cortina.

[Not for nothing did the Lotus name become an acronym of some scorn – LOTUS = Lots of Trouble, Usually Serious ...]

Chapman's masterstroke was to persuade Ford that the car should also be assembled at Cheshunt rather than at Dagenham, though I suspect Dagenham's production chiefs were quite relieved about that:

'Chapman was able to convince Ford,' Harry Calton confirms, 'that because of the many changes that would be necessary, and the complications of the rear suspension, and the aluminium panels and everything else, that Cheshunt was really the only place to assemble the cars.

'The Ford manufacturing people, in any case, were really up to there with the volumes that they were already being asked to build. I think that, as far as they were concerned, there was enough hassle in the press shop, just stamping out the aluminium panels, because the reject rate on those was unreal.

'They were already struggling to meet the schedule of ordinary Cortinas – the last thing they needed was an aluminium-panelled, special-engine, special transmission and suspension variant of the Cortina also going through.

'As long as these cars had the A-frame suspension, I do not believe anybody at Ford Motor Co. would have thought twice about even attempting to build the Lotus-Cortina. I do remember that the first time our Quality Control people came back from Cheshunt, one of them commented: "I don't think they even know what a torque wrench actually is ...!"'

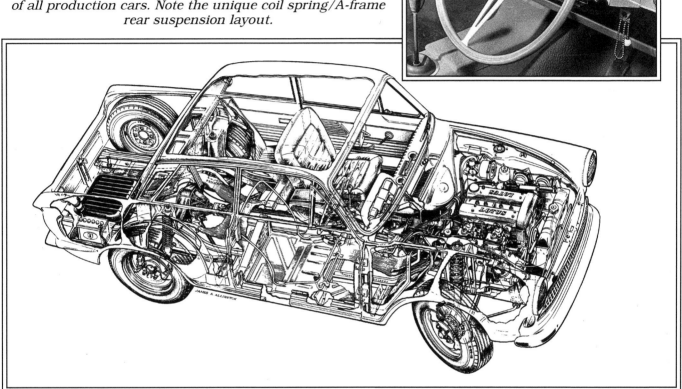

This was the original Lotus-Cortina prototype facia panel, based on the 1962/1963 Cortina instrument layout. It was not carried forward to production cars.

Ford's official Lotus-Cortina cutaway drawing was completed at the end of 1962 before the design was finalised. The drawing, for instance, shows the spare wheel tucked in to the left side of the boot, whereas the wheel was bolted to the floor of all production cars. Note the unique coil spring/A-frame rear suspension layout.

Mk I development – a complete redesign

Chapman's small team, led by Bob Dance and Steve Sanville, took delivery of an early-production white Cortina 1200 two-door in August 1962 – only a month before the Cortina was due to be launched – and began the transformation.

The first Lotus-Cortina was about as different from the 'base' Cortina as it could have been – probably more so than Ford had ever expected, and certainly more than the Product Planning department had hoped. Purely to make the production cars more durable, and more reliable in motorsport, the detail of that design would get progressively less special as the months and years passed.

Starting from a Cortina two-door body shell, Lotus added its own 105bhp twin-cam engine, backed it by a diaphragm spring clutch, a Ford gearbox which used the close-ratio Elan gearbox ratios and a Cortina GT/Capri GT type of remote-control gear shift – which had already been developed for the Elan sportscar, still to be announced) – and fitted transmission assemblies where the light alloy clutch bell housing, gearbox extension and rear axle nose pieces were cast in aluminium instead of cast iron.

At first, the new twin-cam engine could not be fitted, even into the Cortina's spacious engine bay, because the Weber carburettor's inlet trumpets were too long, but 'hacksaw engineering' soon dealt with that problem. The transmission transplants, on the other hand, were straightforward enough, for although the casings were in light alloy, they were the same size as the standard Ford items.

The rear suspension was completely revised, for Lotus arrogantly assumed that Ford's own leaf spring layout could not control rear axle movement accurately, and that severe axle tramp would have been inevitable. Not only were the leaf springs totally discarded (to be replaced by combined coil spring/

damper units which took up the space previously occupied merely by the Cortina's vertical telescopic dampers) but a substantial tubular stiffening structure was added inside the shell to stiffen up the shell mountings for the springs. The whole car sat down a lot lower – 3.5in/89mm – than on ordinary Cortinas, which meant that with four passengers on board there was precious little spring movement or ground clearance to spare.

The axle itself was securely and accurately located by a combination of twin trailing radius arms and what was called an 'A-frame,' which was tied to the axle nose piece and the forward pivot points of the trailing radius arms.

But getting the handling right wasn't easy. Len Terry, who later became one of Lotus's most successful F1 designers, once stated: 'When I got [to Lotus in September 1962] the Lotus-Cortina was nearly finished – and the rear suspension was virtually a copy of my earlier Terrier Mk 2. I told Chapman the car was going to oversteer like a pig, because he'd made the suspension like the

production Terriers, with tubular radius arms, not channel section.

'They took it to Snetterton and, of course, it oversteered. I crowed a bit to Colin, so he said: "If you're so bloody clever, you sort it out." And I did.'

Brakes (front disc and rear drum) were from the soon-to-be-announced Cortina GT, and a Girling vacuum servo was standard.

Other special touches, which were obvious when you opened the boot, were that the spare wheel (much fatter than standard because of the use of 6.00-13in cross-ply tyres on 5.5in rims) was bolted to the boot floor instead of tucked to one side, and the battery had also been relocated to the right side of the boot.

When the prototype car was unveiled in January 1963, incidentally, one pre-launch cutaway drawing which was actually completed for Ford (by James A Allington, whose work appeared regularly in *Autosport*) showed the spare wheel mounted vertically on the left of the boot in the usual Cortina position, while another (by

John Marsden of *Autocar*) showed it bolted flat to the floor. *Motor*, perhaps hedging its bets, did not publish a drawing at all!

Add to this the lowered and stiffened front suspension, which featured lengthened track control arms to give the new car a zero front wheel camber, and a 0.94in/23.8mm diameter anti-roll bar, the 12 per cent more direct steering (due to a revised steering box assembly) plus Elan-type wood-rimmed steering wheel, the 5.5in steel wheel rims and 6.00-section tyres, and one can see that the Lotus-Cortina looked and behaved like a very different car.

Early owners soon found that if the transmission stayed in one piece – and until oil sealing problems in the back axle were sorted out – the original lightweight Lotus-Cortina was one of the very fastest saloon cars on British roads, particularly on a journey where roadholding and response were more important than outright speed.

Inside the car there was a new fascia panel display, using the same basic panel which would be added to 1964-model Cortinas but with different instruments. There were new covers and styling to the seats, and extra padding to the separate front seats. Add to this the use of aluminium door skins, bonnet panel and boot lid panels, along with the special colour scheme, a black grille and the Lotus badges (already-world-famous), and here was a truly distinctive machine.

Even by Lotus standards, the project came together at a staggering speed. The tiny development team, working with virtually no budget, few facilities, only one or two cars, and a fair amount of indifference from Chapman himself (who, apparently, thought that fettling a saloon car was rather below his dignity) somehow managed to turn a great idea into a viable prototype in a matter of months.

Lotus-Cortina on the market

When the press first saw the new model in January 1963, they thought it looked fabulous, especially as features like the new dashboard, remote-control gearchange, low ride height, quarter bumpers and special colour scheme had not been seen on previous models.

Those were the days in which Colin Chapman's genius, and his assurances that the new suspension was necessary were still accepted. Terry Beckett still recalls the launch, when Chapman stood up to address his audience, saying that:

'Of course I've had to do quite a few things to the suspension to get this car going!' – and that there was a roar of laughter from all those who had already decided that the half-elliptic leaf springs were old-fashioned.

The press not only took the car on trust at this time but were very welcoming when road-test cars finally arrived nearly a year later, towards the end of 1963. Roger Bell, who was a junior tester at *Motor* in 1963, stated many years later that there had been a lively debate about the handling:

'Was the technically regressive new rear suspension better on the road than the original one? The test team said "no." We reckoned the A-frame glued the back end down so well, the front always lost grip first, resulting in safe and consistent understeer.

'Too much for extrovert drivers – but at least you knew where you were. Later leaf-spring systems were stronger but less consistent, more prone to sudden tail-end whoopsies that kept you on your toes.

'Characteristically, this car wriggled and writhed like a drunken sidewinder on anything but smooth surfaces, fidgety steering movements being the order if its wanderings were to be kept in check.'

Those were the days in which British motoring magazines were more diplomatic than they are today, so the printed word of January 1964 does not make things quite as clear. Even so, the performance was described as 'striking' – for the recorded top speed was 108mph, with 0-60mph acceleration in a stirring 10.1 seconds. One of the quirks of the original ultra-close ratio gearbox was that the car reached 46mph in bottom gear and 70mph in second!:

'Even the most blasé motorist is likely to find himself seeking an excuse for a dice round the local roads ...'

Autocar initially made a cock-up of its test, being far too gentle with the car and recording 0-60mph in 13.6 seconds (though there was evidence, too, that the engine was out of tune). A swift re-test saw 0-60 recorded in a much more believable 9.9 seconds.

John Bolster, writing in *Autosport*, was surprisingly restrained, and commented that:

'The man who drives mostly in towns or traffic would probably prefer the more flexible GT and would certainly use less petrol. For really going places on the open road, however, the Lotus model, with its fierce acceleration and its speed of well over 100mph, is incomparably the better car and is made to be exploited by the press-on driver.'

All seemed to be well at first, especially as by the end of 1963 Lotus had also produced thirty ultra-special race-tuned versions with Cosworth-prepared 140bhp engines, firmed-up suspension, high-ratio steering boxes, a choice of rear axle ratios and many other

The first Lotus-Cortinas sat much nearer to the ground than any other Cortina, and were easily recognised by their green-on-white colour schemes, black front grilles, wide-rim wheels and Lotus badges on the grille and rear flanks.

Every Lotus-Cortina Mark I was painted white with Lotus-green stripes and panel across the tail. Ford chose Brands Hatch for this shot, intending to remind the world that this was meant to be a racing saloon car.

To improve roadholding, Lotus not only fitted its own design of coil spring/A-frame rear suspension, but also lowered the car considerably. The original Mark I specification featured a number of aluminium body panels.

When Ford introduced the aeroflow 'facelift' Cortina in the autumn of 1964, the Lotus-Cortina fascia layout was also altered. The 1965 and 1966 model year cars had this layout, with more instruments in a very neat display.

For 1965 and 1966, the Lotus-Cortina received a wide-mouth black front grille (and the 'CORTINA' motif on the bonnet) but other styling features were not changed.

special fittings. For these cars (and depending on the axle ratio used) Lotus claimed a top speed of more than 135mph.

But all was not well for it wasn't long before the first warranty claims began to flood in – the persistent failure of rear axles being endemic at first. This, incidentally, was due to the way the A-frame tugged and nagged away at the centre of the rear axle, which encouraged fixing nuts to loosen, the oil to drain away and the crown-wheel-and-pinion to fail.

Sports Editor of *Autocar*, Peter Garnier, ran an early car from May 1963 for no less than 29,000 miles, eventually losing all patience with it. In two years there were no fewer than six rear-axle failures, not to mention at least three rear-suspension failures – all these problems being directly related to the Lotus redesign. This was typical of early owners' experiences, so something, it was clear, had to be done.

Until then, Ford had always taken a rather semi-detached, arms-length attitude to the new model. Ford supplied white-painted, two-door Cortina shells from Dagenham to the Lotus factory at Cheshunt, together with other chassis components which were still common to the existing Cortina GT (brakes, some suspension and steering components, the fuel tank, for instance). Ford then left assembly of the cars to Lotus.

At the factory Lotus added the famous green paint spears along the flanks, which blended smoothly into the green rear panel, after which the cars were built up at Cheshunt – in assembly shops already bursting at the seams – before being delivered back to Ford, where they were plugged into the normal Ford distribution system.

1963	228 cars
1964	563 cars
1965	1112 cars
1966	991 cars

Coil-spring cars:
1100 cars (approximately)
Leaf-spring cars:
1800 cars (approximately)

Delivery, in any numbers, didn't begin until the summer of '63, and were limited in the first year. (They couldn't begin, in any case, until Ford could supply the Cortina GT chassis components, and that car did not get into the Ford showrooms until April 1963.)

When Lotus revealed the limited edition (of thirty) 140bhp Group 2 cars at the end of the year, it claimed that 'the normal 105bhp cars are coming off the line at Cheshunt at the rate of five per day.' This was PR nonsense, as we now know, for figures released in the 1980s show that just 228 cars were produced in the calendar year 1963.

Today's Lotus-Cortina enthusiasts tell me that the original A-frame cars are now the most desirable, yet the combined shock/spring mountings always gave the shell a hard time, which resulted in kinks appearing in that area (until Lotus beefed up the stiffening arrangements).

At first Ford was unalarmed about the problems. To quote Harry Calton:

'It started racing and winning in September 1963, and it marched over everything in sight, and that was enough. We could keep on saying: "But it's winning, it's winning ..." and the people who bought them were ready to live with all the problems.

'Reliability usually wasn't an issue as far as they were concerned

... when it was running, and it was on song, it was super, and that seemed to be enough.

'The dealers lived with this – they learned to live with this.'

In the first two years, therefore, many changes were forced through, some not made public. Special Equipment cars had 115bhp engines, and were little publicised at the time. From July 1964 a two-piece propeller shaft took over from the one-piece, most of the light-alloy panels and castings were abandoned, and a wider set of gearbox ratios was fitted. Then, from October 1964, the latest 'Aeroflow' type of body shell was standardised, with full-width grille and through-flow ventilation.

Next, in June 1965, came the most important change of all. The A-frame suspension was abandoned in favour of the Cortina GT's leaf spring + radius arm setup, which offended Lotus fanatics but proved to be surprisingly effective.

Colin Chapman, in fact, was violently opposed to this, so Ford arranged to run back-to-back tests at Snetterton with Vic Elford and Jack Sears. Sears, in particular, was considerably quicker with the leaf-spring version, and that really clinched the reason for change.

Finally, from October 1965, yet another set of gearbox ratios was used, those being the 'Corsair 2000E' ratios which would eventually be standardised for the Cortina GT Mk II. This, incidentally, was also the

first time left-hand-drive versions were officially built.

Because the Cortina was about to be restyled, and because Lotus was planning to move its entire centre of operations to Hethel in Norfolk, the last of 2894 original-shape Lotus-Cortinas were produced at Cheshunt in the autumn of 1966. Year-on-year production was as shown in the table.

This means, for sure, that the later 'leaf-spring' Mk I car was much more saleable than the earlier 'coil spring' cars. As the appropriate Cheshunt chassis records have now been mislaid, no-one seems to have an accurate breakdown of production numbers.

However, since the 'leaf-spring' car went into production in mid-1965, and was obviously a success (most importantly, Ford *and* the dealer chain trusted it more than they had ever trusted the coil-spring variety) I would guess at the breakdown of numbers shown in the table.

As the years passed, many coil spring cars were converted by their later owners to the leaf-spring specification but then, to confound all logic, I believe that a number of those cars were reconverted to coil spring specification in the 1990s to make them more 'authentic.'

Lotus-Cortina Mk II: better, but not as special

After the Mk I model was discontinued, there was then a six-

The Lotus-Ford Twin-Cam engine was wide, and only just fitted into the engine bay of the Mark II body shell. This explains the slim shape of the air collector linking the air cleaner (atop the camshaft covers) and the twin-choke Weber carburettors.

month gap with no Lotus-Cortinas on the market. This explains why the 'works' rally team used out-of-production Mk Is to win the RAC rally of November 1966, and the Swedish rally of February 1967.

It was only in March 1967 that Ford was ready to announce the Lotus-Cortina Mk II, which was a very different car in many ways. Not only was it based on the structure of the new-shape Cortina Mk II, but the company now proposed to build all the cars at Dagenham, among other Mk II-shape Cortinas, rather than at Lotus, where the build quality failings had often dismayed Ford (to put it very politely indeed).

Even though the last of the Mark Is – the 'leaf-spring' cars – had been much better than the originals, they still did not come up to Ford's own self-imposed standards. By all accounts, Lotus had made a lot of money out of building Lotus-Cortinas at Cheshunt, so Colin Chapman was understandably furious when he lost the Mk II build contract.

For Ford, nevertheless, it was a real blessing. Not only was the new version a much more conventional model in many ways, also it was more reliable and – as it transpired – assembled with more care. Since Lotus was in the process of moving its factory more than a hundred miles – from Cheshunt to Hethel Airfield (near Norfolk) – this was probably wise.

Having driven lots of Lotus-Cortinas when they were current cars, I've never understood why the Mk II has tended to be 'talked down' in later years. In almost every way except outright straight-line speed, it was a better car than the Mk I – better-built and better-equipped – with a more roomy cabin.

There wasn't any doubt, though, that some of the character had gone missing in the move back to Dagenham. What was really a twin-cam-engined Mk II GT somehow lacked the charisma of a Mk I, even if you knew the axle wasn't going to let you down, and that you would usually reach your destination, far or near!

A Lotus-Cortina Mk II shared the same rounded, two-door, appearance of the new-style Cortina GT, the same basic mechanical layout, fascia style and leaf-spring/radius-arm layout, and could be ordered in a whole range of monochrome colours. On customer demand, a contrasting 'speed stripe' could be added in the Ford dealer's paint shop. (This was, in fact, done to all of Ford's own press and factory demonstration models.)

As produced on the Dagenham assembly lines, none of these cars had aluminium body panels, or light-alloy transmission casings, though Ford made sure that these were homologated as options for use in motorsport.

For the Mk II the 1558cc Lotus twin-cam engine was in Special Equipment guise, quoted by Lotus at 115bhp, but by Ford as 109bhp (net) and was almost identical to the unit fitted to the Escort Twin-Cam which went on sale in 1968. As with the last Mk Is, the gearbox had 2000E/Mk II GT ratios, but the axle ratio was higher this time – 3.77:1 instead of 3.90:1.

As before, all cars had lowered and stiffened suspension and 5.5in wide-rim steel wheels, for the very first time with 165-13in radial ply tyres. The spare wheel was mounted upright at the side of the boot compartment, but the battery still had its own tray on the boot floor.

Far more Mk IIs were made than Mk Is – Ford claims 4032 examples – and these were in production until July 1970, but the steam really went out of the programme after the Escort Twin-Cam went on sale in mid-1968, as many enthusiasts turned to that car instead. To relate it even more closely to the Escort Twin-Cam, by the end of 1967 Ford had begun adding 'Twin Cam' badges to the boot lid – and removing the 'Lotus' roundels from the cross panel. Ford even went so far as to register a number of racecars and demonstrators in the 'CTC ... E' sequence – where CTC, of course, meant 'Cortina Twin Cam.'

The impetus behind the Lotus-Cortina had gone by 1969 – it was no longer being used in front-line races or rallies – which meant that only 194 cars were built in 1970.

In those three years, important

In some ways the Lotus-Cortina Mark II was less of a thoroughbred, but a more reliable sports saloon. Based on the Mark II two-door shell, it had all-steel body panels, and the striping was optional, not standard.

From the full side view there's no doubt that the Mark II Lotus-Cortina rode at a similar height to every other Mark II. The ACBC Lotus badges on the rear flanks close to the tail lamps give the game away.

Below: 'I've seen the Lions of Longleat.' Do you remember that safari park slogan of the 1960s? Ford thought it made a good talking point for the new Lotus-Cortina style.

Below-The Lotus-Cortina Mark II's style was less extrovert than that of the Mark I, though the black grille and the 5.5in wheel rims remained. Cars were available in a full range of body colours, the stripes (if any) being added by dealers at a customer's request.

Mk II changes were limited to a new fascia/instrument panel layout from October 1968 (all other Cortinas got the change at the same time) and a new type of 'single-rail' remote-control gearshift, plus a centre-floor mounted handbrake, from that point.

Temperament ... or reliability?
So, which type do *you* want? Classic car values suggest that the Mk II has always been the poor relation, yet there are more of them available, some in remarkably good condition. Do you have the patience to put up with the well-charted vagaries of an early Mk I example and the fragility of the aluminium panels?

On the other hand, would you rather go almost as quickly in a Mk II, remembering that, in 1967, *Motor* magazine testers suggested that: 'Anyone in the market for a

The 1969-70 versions of the Lotus-Cortina (badged as Twin-Cams) used this derivative of the corporate fascia/instrument panel, with a padded steering wheel hub, which was similar to the 1600E display but had a fabric covered panel.

This Ford publicity shot points out the Lotus-Cortina's links with motorsport, for the car is parked next to a Lotus F2 car, complete with Cosworth Ford FVA engine, and that is a Superspeed racing Anglia 105E on the ramps.

From this angle, and with the optional stripes added, there's no doubt that this was a Lotus-Cortina, although it didn't ride as low as the original type, and there was no boot-lid badging at first. (Later cars were badged 'CORTINA TWIN-CAM' on the boot lid.)

£1100 saloon who doesn't buy a Lotus-Cortina must be mad ...'?

I was personally responsible for the *Autocar* road test published in August 1967 so I am happy to quote my own words from the opening summary:

'With the latest product of Ford's association with Lotus, the Cortina retains much of its dynamic performance, yet is so much more refined than the earlier car that there is scarcely any comparison between them. It is immensely better, and is now a thoroughly satisfying high-performance car.'

Now, go away and argue among yourselves ...

4

THE 'WORKS' CORTINAS – RACING AND RALLYING

This is a story – of racing, rallying and an enormous amount of international success – that covers six years. In that short period, a whole variety of Cortina and Lotus-Cortinas won events as varied as European saloon car championships and the East African Safari, winning on tarmac, rough roads, on ice, snow, and in blazing desert conditions. Heroes like Jim Clark and Roger Clark took the wheel ... what more is there to say?

The Cortina motorsport story really began in mid-1962, when Walter Hayes arrived at Ford and soon introduced an ambitious new motorsport strategy – which didn't come a moment too soon. For years Ford's 'works' team had relied on Zephyrs (which were too large) or on Anglias (which were too slow).

Hayes did not like to see Ford's big rivals, BMC, winning all the events and scooping all the headlines. He immediately put in hand a programme geared towards domination of saloon-car racing and success in world-class rallies.

Hayes knew that the new Cortina was due to be launched later that year, and that a high-performance GT model would follow in 1963. Not satisfied with that, he also called up his old friend Colin Chapman of Lotus, confirming that an even more exciting version (which Chapman had already discussed with Patrick Hennessy and Terry Beckett) should be campaigned.

According to the newly developed Hayes master plan, the 'works' team would be relocated to a new workshop at Boreham in 1963, the Lotus-Cortina would be homologated soon afterwards and would become Ford's front-line competition car. Scores of special 'homologation' items would be developed and made available to private owners. It was all very novel and very exciting.

It was a great plan – but it fell apart at the first obstacle. The Lotus-Cortina, though announced in January 1963, was slow to go on sale. Early examples proved remarkably fragile as racecars, and as soon as they took to rough roads their rear suspension broke with monotonous regularity. Enter Master Plan Mark Two ... the Cortina GT was speedily developed as a rally car while the Lotus-Cortina became a racecar.

Since the saga began with rally cars and with the Cortina GTs, I have detailed their career first. The Lotus-Cortina's illustrious racing career follows towards the end of this chapter.

Cortina GT – early development

Over the years, I've always thought that the original Cortina GTs were Ford's most underestimated 'works' rally cars. Without the development of the GTs, other world-beating models – such as the Lotus-Cortinas and Escort Twin-Cams – might

The very first 'works' Cortina entry in motorsport was driven by Jeff Uren (holding homologation papers) on the 1962 RAC Rally.

TOO 528 was the original 'works' Cortina for motorsport, a much-modified 1200 model driven by Jeff Uren, here seen (close to the door opening) talking to Laurie Hands of Champion Sparking Plugs.

never have been as famous. *Any car which can win the East African Safari and the Touring Car category of the Alpine rally has to be a superlative machine.*

The first 'works' Cortina to go rallying, in the 1962 RAC, was Jeff Uren's highly tuned 1200 (though that car hit all manner of problems). Team leader Henry Taylor's Monte

outing in 1963, also in a 1200, then resulted in second in class.

For 1963, team manager Sid Henson hired three new drivers – Pat Moss, David Seigle-Morris and Peter Riley – all of whom had defected from BMC (where the cars were faster but the driving fees were lower). If they couldn't deliver, who on earth could?

Immediately after the GT was introduced, a team was sent to tackle the East African Safari, but every team member dropped out. On the Tulip which followed, Pat Moss struggled against unfavourable handicaps, so it wasn't until May and the hot, rough and dusty Acropolis, that the GTs made a show.

By this time the Cortina production car was acquiring a reputation as a car which was quite amazingly light for its bulk. Know-alls naturally assumed that this would make the body too flimsy to withstand rough-road events. They were wrong. However, everyone was surprised to see Henry Taylor and Pat Moss finish in the top six, especially as they were only beaten by Mercedes-Benz and Volvo saloons, both of which were acknowledged rough-road 'tanks.' It was a great performance, which made all the private owners jealous – and puzzled.

TOO 528 made its second 'works' rallying appearance in the 1963 Monte Carlo rally where, driven by Henry Taylor and Brian Melia, it was engulfed in blizzard conditions.

Bill Barnett, always the deputy but never Ford's competitions boss, was the organising genius behind every 'works' Cortina rallying effort in the 1960s.

In 1963 the first series of 'works' Cortina GTs used this triangular display of Cibie driving lamps, and Land-Rover-type bonnet security straps.

The reason? British drivers already knew that the original GT two-door body shells seemed to be very fragile. The first time I co-drove a Cortina GT in 1963, my driver (Phil Simister) noticed that the body shell had started to distort after only one night's rough-road motoring in Welsh lanes. After only 300 miles there was a slight but definite crease across the roof between the door pillars, along with other creases over the rear wheelarches. A lot of stiffening and buttressing was needed to stop that happening again.

In the meantime, Henson's assistant, Bill Barnett, had homologated many extra items,

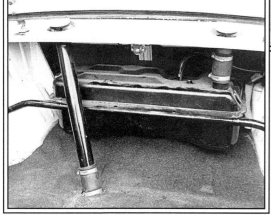

One of Ford's most popular motorsport options for Cortinas was this auxiliary petrol tank mounting: the tank was positioned inside the boot, above the line of the back axle.

and others were added in the next two years. Extra fuel tanks, wide-rimmed wheels and alternative gear ratios were all approved, but after reading FIA Appendix J regulations, no-one could ever understand how an engine with twin dual-choke Weber carburettors came to be listed in the Group 1 'showroom' category when 5000 units were supposed to have been made!

It was no wonder that the cars were competitive – in rallies and on the race track – for these Weber-equipped engines developed around 110bhp, compared to the 78bhp of the standard car. Better not to ask about fuel consumption, however ...

Success at last
After mid-63, when Bo Ljungfeldt's Swedish-registered car finished third overall in the Midnight Sun Rally (behind a Porsche Super 90, and Erik Carlsson's Saab) and Henry Taylor's car finished third on the Alpine (behind a Mini-Cooper S and an Alfa Romeo Tubolare

The 'works' Cortina GTs of 1964 used this complex array of instruments, switches and controls.

A full team of 'works' Cortina GTs tackled the 1964 RAC Rally. David Seigle Morris is driving 889 DOO on the way to ninth place; his team-mate, Vic Elford, finished third overall.

In 1964 and 1965 Vic Elford was Ford's fastest 'works' rally driver. Here, during the 1964 Alpine Rally, he takes a rest while co-driver David Stone drives the red Cortina GT.

TZ) it was suddenly clear that the Cortina had become a rugged and formidable machine.

Even so, because of its very powerful engine, everyone at Ford wanted to see the Lotus-Cortina in rallies. With that in mind, Taylor's regular team car (a Cortina GT, 888 DOO) was given a Lotus engine for the ultra-tough Spa-Sofia-Liège Rally, where the regulations were very liberal. Somehow or other,

the engine coped with the awful Yugoslavian and Bulgarian fuel, the car held together for four days, and Taylor took fourth place.

For 1964 it was all-change time at Boreham. Sid Henson left the team, and Alan Platt took his place as Competition Manager. Pat Moss moved on to Saab – although there was a moment when her new husband, Erik Carlsson, nearly

signed for Ford, in which case she would not have left the team – and Vic Elford arrived, having made his name in 1963 with Triumph.

Boreham retained the same set of registration plates – 888 DOO to 893 DOO inclusive – but threw away the old white body shells in favour of a new set of red ones. Not

Ford's 'works' team of red Cortina GTs won the Manufacturers' Team Prize in the 1964 RAC Rally, driven by Vic Elford (893 DOO) Henry Taylor (888 DOO) and David Seigle-Morris (889 DOO). Here they are seen on the Snetterton special test.

that this helped the team in Monte Carlo, where some mechanical problems intervened.

Safari victory

Another brand-new set of white cars was built for the 1964 East African Safari, where – in an absolutely brilliant performance – the cars not only won outright and took third place, but won the Manufacturers' Team Prize. This was the sort of result advertising departments dream about, and it did great things for morale at Boreham. Peter Hughes (Kenyan resident and also the Ford importer) drove the winning car (KHS 600) and no fewer than four of the six team cars made it to the finish.

The members of the team now knew that they could always finish well up, and be especially competitive on rough events; however, they were frustrated by the lack of horsepower. The Lotus twin-cams could push out 140/150bhp without any reliability problems, but their chassis were not yet strong enough for rallying.

The cars could either be prepared to ride low and handle well, or to sit high on raised suspension, well clear of the rocks of a Safari, a Liège or an RAC stage. They were, of course, ideally

'disposable' rally machines, for if a body shell got crumpled (and several did) they were immediately thrown away and replaced by new ones. As far as I know, no 1964-65 team cars were sold on for private owners to use in rallying; they were simply scrapped. Certainly none has survived.

The team performance on the French Alpine of 1964 – an event which every current 'works' driver thought to be the most demanding of all – established the legend for good. After the first night, David Seigle-Morris's car was ahead of Vic Elford's sister car, to lead the Touring Car category, and even though Seigle-Morris half-rolled his car on the Col du Rousset test, he held on to that lead for three more days.

Then, only twenty-five miles from the finish of the event, David's car blew a cylinder head gasket, handing victory to team-mate Vic Elford instead. Ford's advertising used to claim that: 'You can buy the same Cortina ...' which was close, but not *that* close, to the truth. It would help if you could interpret an homologation form, and knew that Henry Taylor's co-driver, Brian Melia, was also involved in selling parts to private owners.

All the team drivers retired on

the last of the great Spa-Sofia-Liège Marathons, but they shrugged that off later in the year. (In that particular event the entry included a Lotus-engined Corsair, which David Seigle-Morris inverted.)

Back in Britain in the RAC Rally, the red Cortina GTs came close to victory, but Vic Elford's phenomenal run was marred by off-track excursions. Eventually he finished third, none too pleased with himself, while David Seigle-Morris languished in eighth place. Even so, the team won the Manufacturers' Prize again.

For 1965 the 'works' team knew that the leaf-spring Lotus-Cortina was on the way, which they believed to be a car guaranteed to cure all their frustrations; for the time being, the same team of 1964-vintage red Cortina GTs (suitably re-shelled whenever they got damaged) was retained.

In the meantime, a young man from Leicester, Roger Clark, had prepared his own Cortina GT, originally as a private entry, and later with factory assistance. In 1964 the new car had won the Scottish Rally outright; then in 1965, and in a matter of weeks it finished third on the Circuit of Ireland, won the Scottish Rally and went on to win the Gulf London

Before he started driving for the 'works' Ford team, Roger Clark twice won the Scottish Rally in his own self-prepared Cortina GTs, and this picture is from the 1965 event. His car has recently lost one of its extra driving lamps. Watching his progress is Ford co-driver/administrator Brian Melia (extreme right, partly obscured by the dust cloud).

Roger Clark was Ford's – and Britain's – most successful rally driver in the 1960s and 1970s. Before becoming 'Mr Escort' he notched up an impressive number of Cortina successes.

International. Was it any wonder that Roger was swiftly swept into the 'works' team, where he would stay for the next fifteen years?

The team's last full outing with this model came in the East African Safari, when the cars were driven by Kenyan crews. Perhaps it was too much to expect them to repeat their 1964 success, for the best that could be achieved was third overall, with another team car down in ninth place, a further four *hours* (not minutes!) adrift. As a finale, Henry Taylor then travelled to Canada for the Shell 4000 event where, in a GT entered by the factory, he finished second overall behind a Ford Mustang.

When a brand-new team of white 'works' leaf-sprung Lotus-Cortinas turned up on the French Alpine Rally in June 1965, we all knew that the Cortina GT's rally career was virtually over. As far as Boreham was concerned, the team had no further use for the push-rod-engined GTs, but they were still great favourites with private owners until the end of production in 1966.

If the new-shape Lotus-Cortina Mk II had appeared a few months earlier, it could have been homologated for all 1967 events,

but because of the five-month delay, the Cortina GT Mk II was also used once by the 'works' rally team – in the Safari at Eastertide in that year. Bengt Söderström's car led the event for many hours until it crashed; team-mate Jack Simonian took over from him before hitting a large animal; Peter Hughes went on to finish third overall.

Lotus-Cortinas in rallying

For knowledgeable Cortina owners, what follows might seem an unlikely story. How could a car as fragile as the original Lotus-Cortina eventually be transformed into a rugged, bomb-proof rally car?

The answer, in a word, is 'Boreham.' If the motorsport department had not needed a successor to the Cortina GT, and had not been determined to prove something with the Lotus-Cortina, it might never have happened. Even so, it took Boreham three years to get everything right – and it was only an emphatic victory in the 1966 RAC Rally which proved the point.

The incentive, quite simply, was that the 'works' Cortina GTs didn't have enough power to go on winning rallies outright, so the Lotus-Cortinas had to be made to do that instead. Once the Lotus was made

reliable, it was always competitive, and always likely to win.

I'm highlighting the Lotus-Cortina's rallying career because it tends to sink without trace in the nostalgia surrounding Escorts. Yet, at the time, no-one was allowed to ignore it, for the Lotus-Cortina was Ford's 'works' rallying mainstay for three busy years, and there was even a short, headline-making overlap with the Escort after the smaller car had been launched.

But it wasn't all good news. In 1963 and 1964 it was agreed that anyone who entered a Lotus-Cortina for a rally needed his head examining, and a fleet of service cars to follow him around; even at the end, in 1968, an engine failure could often spoil the master plan.

Yet let's not forget that the Lotus-Cortina was eventually a rally car which won major events like the RAC Rally, the Swedish Rally, the Shell 4000 Rally, the Scottish Rally, the Gulf London Rally ... and which so nearly won several other big events in 1966 and 1967, and the London-Sydney Marathon of 1968.

Not meant to be a rally car

As the 'father' of the Lotus-Cortina, Walter Hayes wanted it to be a special, limited production car to start winning saloon car races. There was little mention – and certainly no prior intention – of using such a machine as a rally car.

The Lotus-Cortina was previewed in January 1963, well before it went on sale, and homologation followed later in the year. [Homologation into Group 2, according to the regulations, required 1000 cars to be produced, but we now know that Lotus only built 228 cars in the whole of 1963 ... rules? what rules?]

According to the record books, the first 'works' Lotus-Cortina to go rallying was driven by Henry Taylor and Brian Melia in the long, rough and very rugged Spa-Sofia-Liège Rally of September 1963 – but this is quite untrue. In fact, this car was Henry's regular Cortina GT – 888 DOO – complete with conventional leaf-spring rear suspension, which had already competed in the Acropolis and French Alpine events.

This time, for an event where the regulations were very relaxed, a lightly tuned Lotus-Cortina engine was installed and the experienced crew nursed the car home into fourth place. If nothing else, it proved that a Lotus-Cortina with a durable chassis might also become a great rally car.

This, in fact, was the start of a long development and proving programme. To see if the model in its original specification could be made rally-worthy, Taylor and his regular co-driver Brian Melia then used a genuine 'works' Lotus-Cortina (786 BOO) on the 1963 RAC Rally, complete with A-bracket rear suspension, lightweight panels and alloy gearbox casing. It was a very traumatic rally for everyone, although they managed to finish sixth.

Team manager Bill Barnett recalled that the drivers '... almost had to carry it to the finish. I reckon we changed something, or welded up that blasted rear end, at every available garage in Wales and Scotland.'

That was enough to prove to Boreham that the A-bracket suspension would never work on rough rallies. But could it be made to work on long-distance tarmac events? The chance to find out came in September 1964, when Vic Elford and David Seigle-Morris took a new car (ETW 362B) on the ten-day, 4000-mile Tour de France, an all-tarmac event which included eight one-hour races, lots of speed

Vic Elford and David Stone in one of the well-known team of 'KPU...C' factory-prepared Lotus-Cortinas, halfway up the Mont Ventoux hill climb of the 1966 Alpine Rally. By any standards, Vic was the fastest 'tarmac' driver in the Ford team – and certainly the most unlucky.

Inset – Roger Clark's fine drive in the 1966 Monte Carlo Rally (when he should have been credited with fourth overall in this Group 1 Lotus-Cortina) was spoiled by the fiasco of disqualification for an alleged lighting infringement.

Scottish Rally 1966: hot weather and dusty special stages. Roger Clark and Brian Melia enjoying their 'works' Lotus-Cortina. (On this occasion it retired with a broken back axle.)

On one famous occasion, double F1 World Champion Jim Clark competed in the RAC rally. Using this 'works' Lotus-Cortina, and partnered by Brian Melia, he set a whole series of fastest stage times before retiring after a major accident. Jim loved every minute of it – and so did the spectators!

The 'works' Lotus-Cortina's most emphatic rally victory came in the 1966 RAC Rally, when Bengt Söderström and Gunnar Palm won the event by nearly fourteen minutes.

hill climbs in the French Alps and a good deal of high-speed rallying around twisty mountain roads in the Alpes Maritimes.

It took several service car teams to keep the car going, as on the RAC Rally entry of 1963, but this time the car revelled in the conditions, finishing fourth overall in the Touring Car category (behind two Ford Mustangs and a Jaguar 3.8 Mk 2) and winning the prestigious Handicap category outright. Not only that, but it was very fast, looked wonderfully stable on the stages – and brought smiles to the faces of its experienced crew.

Front-line 'works' cars

By this time Ford's design engineers had decided to impose Cortina GT-style rear suspension on to the Lotus-Cortina – which meant using leaf springs and radius arms. This meant that, with the exception of the twin-cam engine, the running gear would all be thoroughly familiar to the 'works' rally team at Boreham.

By the end of 1964 the rally team had already committed its immediate future to proving the Lotus-Cortina, knew that the

revised car would go on sale in June 1965, and planned to start rallying it immediately after that. Even in 'long-distance' guise the 1.6-litre engine could produce an easy and (usually) reliable 140bhp, which was at least 30bhp more than the Cortina GTs had.

In their very first event, four cars started in the Alpine Rally of July 1965. Vic Elford's car led the event outright for days, and was never headed – until, less than an hour from the finish, a tiny piece of the engine's distributor fell out on a speed test, stranding him for twenty-six minutes! For Ford, it was really no consolation that Henry Taylor's team car then finished third in the Touring Car category, just 102 seconds off the winning pace.

The RAC Rally was also a great disappointment to the team, as there was heavy snow and all four cars retired. In fact, it was Roger Clark, using a loaned car from Boreham, who gave the Lotus-Cortina its first big rally victory by winning the Welsh International in December 1965. (I can vouch for the lad's genius, and the speed of the car, as I was sitting alongside him on that event as his co-driver.)

Somehow the Lotus-Cortina was re-homologated into Group 1 for 1966 (which means that someone convinced the RAC that 5000 cars had been built in 1965 – a likely story!). Theoretically, this meant that the cars should have won event after event thereafter, but there always seemed to be something (fate, scrutineers, or sheer damned hard luck ...) to frustrate the team. As it happened, there was only one undisputed and emphatic victory during the year – by Bengt Söderström/Gunnar Palm in the RAC Rally – and the cars' unreliability was a major reason for Vic Elford deciding to leave the team.

In the Monte, which was confined to Group 1 cars, Roger Clark's provisional fourth place (behind three 'works' Mini-Cooper S cars) was annulled when he was disqualified in the 'lighting fiasco' which also eliminated the 'works' Minis. Organisers and competitors disagreed on the sporting legality of new-technology quartz-halogen headlamps, which could not be dipped, and victory was quite undeservedly handed to Citroën instead.

Roger Clark and Jim Porter easily won the 1967 Scottish Rally in this 'works' Lotus-Cortina Mark II. At one point in the event Clark jumped the car so high that it creased the shell ahead of the screen earning it the nickname of 'the banana.'

Bengt Söderström was one of the most successful 'works' drivers with Lotus-Cortinas of both shapes – here seen on the snow and ice of the Swedish Rally of 1968.

A few weeks later Vic Elford won the San Remo event on the road, only to be disqualified in the after-rally scrutineering bay when his car's gearbox internals were found to differ from the homologation papers. The papers were wrong – the number of teeth on one gear having been mis-stated – but the Italian scrutineers were not impressed. In later years, when Lancia made similar mistakes, it was all smiles and shrugs and rules were waived ...

Elford then finished second in the Tulip Rally to Rauno Aaltonen's Mini-Cooper S, but thought he would have won if the car had been consistently healthy (the engine suffered an intermittent misfire). Bengt Söderström really finished second in the rough-and-tough Acropolis Rally, only to be handed victory when the winner (Paddy Hopkirk's Mini-Cooper S) was disqualified for a service infringement.

Three brand-new cars tackled the French Alpine, where the cars were expected to at least match the pace of the lightweight Alfa Romeo GTAs. Vic Elford's car blew its engine while leading, while Roger

Clark carried on to finish second overall. It was that sort of year, and the twin-cam engine's durability problems were never really solved until the Escort came along ...

Then came the RAC Rally, a long and arduous event, and four of the cars started. Jim Clark, F1 World Champion, drove with phenomenal speed, but erratically, until he finally crashed the car hard for the second time. It was the fat and placid Swede, Bengt Söderström, who finally won outright by more than thirteen minutes.

Although the model had now dropped out of production, there was to be one more victory for the Mark I car in its original shape – by Söderström, again, in the snowy Swedish Rally of February 1967 – before the team turned to the new-shape Mk II cars (which appeared in March 1967).

Roger Clark made the early headlines, first by winning the Canadian Shell 4000 Rally (with a local co-driver). He trekked all the way across that vast continent for 4000 miles (hence the rally title); then won the hot and dusty Scottish Rally in a car which actually bent its body shell during the event,

and was instantly nicknamed 'The Banana.'

In the meantime, Bengt Söderström finished third in the Acropolis – Paddy Hopkirk's Mini-Cooper S wreaking revenge for 1966 – after which Ove Andersson used the same, but re-prepared, car a few weeks later, to win the incredibly long and tiring Gulf London 'forestry marathon' Rally outright.

Later in the year, the team came very close to winning the Three Cities event (Munich, Vienna and Budapest) when Söderström's car led until the last circuit test, whereupon the clutch exploded, forcing him into second place.

By this time the team, and its drivers, knew that a new and smaller car – the Escort Twin-Cam – was on the way for 1968, and the Lotus-Cortina was almost ready for retirement.

At the end of the year, though, there were high hopes of a storming performance in the RAC Rally, for which no fewer than six 'works' cars were prepared, two of them (for Clark and Söderström) being fuel-injected. This, alas, was the year in which a nationwide outbreak of foot-and-mouth disease caused

During the 1960s, Ford Motorsport developed an enormous range of competition parts for the Cortinas and Lotus-Cortinas. This 1967 study shows a Cortina GT Mark II, and items as various as aluminium body panels, engine tuning parts, special transmission pieces, lightweight seats, skid plates, suspension items and Minilite wheels.

Beautifully balanced in a tail-out slide on the Karlstad trotting track in the 1968 Swedish Rally is the 'works' Lotus-Cortina Mark II of Bengt Söderström/Gunnar Palm. Complete with homologated fuel injection, this car finished fourth overall.

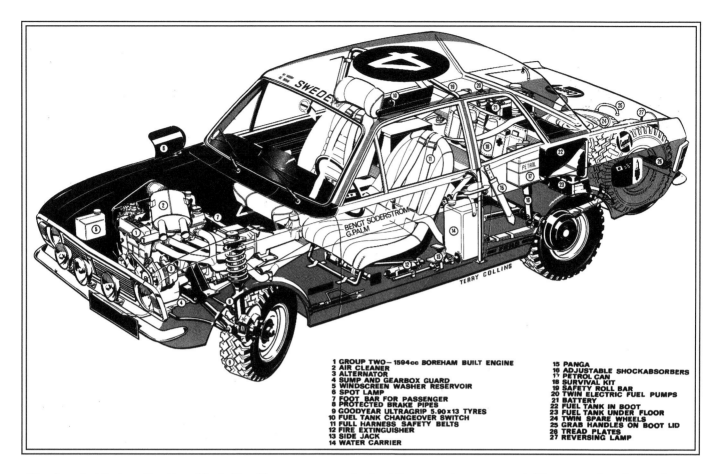

1 GROUP TWO— 1594cc BOREHAM BUILT ENGINE
2 AIR CLEANER
3 ALTERNATOR
4 SUMP AND GEARBOX GUARD
5 WINDSCREEN WASHER RESERVOIR
6 SPOT LAMP
7 FOOT BAR FOR PASSENGER
8 PROTECTED BRAKE PIPES
9 GOODYEAR ULTRAGRIP 5.90 x 13 TYRES
10 FUEL TANK CHANGEOVER SWITCH
11 FULL HARNESS SAFETY BELTS
12 FIRE EXTINGUISHER
13 SIDE JACK
14 WATER CARRIER

15 PANGA
16 ADJUSTABLE SHOCKABSORBERS
17 PETROL CAN
18 SURVIVAL KIT
19 SAFETY ROLL BAR
20 TWIN ELECTRIC FUEL PUMPS
21 BATTERY
22 FUEL TANK IN BOOT
23 FUEL TANK UNDER FLOOR
24 TWIN SPARE WHEELS
25 GRAB HANDLES ON BOOT LID
26 TREAD PLATES
27 REVERSING LAMP

The 'works' Lotus-Cortina Mark II rally car was packed with special equipment. This was the ghosted view of Bengt Söderström's 1968 Safari Rally car.

the rally to be cancelled at twelve hours' notice.

Rallying swansong

As soon as the Escorts were homologated in March 1968, the Lotus-Cortinas were pensioned off, except for two long-distance special cases – the East African Safari, and the London-Sydney Marathon of November-December 1968.

Although a full team of cars was sent to Kenya for the Safari, all but one of them faded before the end, that of local man Peter Huth, who kept going to finish second. The Lotus-Cortina, in fact, seemed to finish second any number of times in its rallying career! It was ironic that the Cortina GTs, with less than 100bhp at the time, should dominate the Safari in 1964, yet

the much more powerful Lotus-Cortinas never came close in later years.

Originally Ford planned to send only two cars on the very first round-the-world adventure – London to Sydney, by way of Bombay and the high seas – but in the end no fewer than five new machines were built, of which the hot favourite was the car to be shared by Roger Clark and Ove Andersson.

As forecast, this car duly led the entire event on the ten-day slog to Bombay (no night halts, please note ....) and it then set out on the four-day dash across Australia, from Perth to Sydney, with every hope of a comfortable victory.

Except that, as so often with Ford models using the twin-cam Lotus engine, it all went wrong

again. Clark's car sped all the way across the hot and dusty Nullabor desert without problems, but then the engine burnt a piston on the way to the Quorn control. Although Eric Jackson's sister car was then called in for the cylinder heads to be swapped over (perhaps ruining Eric's chances of finishing as high as third) there was more misery to come for Clark. On the final night, in the hills west of Sydney, the Lotus-Cortina's axle failed.

Could the Lotus-Cortina have been made even better if the Escort Twin-Cam had not arrived? Of course it could, for – as Roger Clark once told me – it wasn't perfect:

'You know, you could do anything with a Lotus-Cortina in a forest, anything at all – but when you got it sideways it began

When Roger Clark and Ove Andersson left the Perth (Western Australia) control of the 1968 London-Sydney Marathon, they were leading the event and favourites to win, but an engine problem, followed by rear-axle failure, cost them dearly.

It is 3.30pm and the 'works' Lotus-Cortina of Roger Clark and Ove Andersson crosses Westminster Bridge shortly after the start of the 1968 London to Sydney Marathon.

to feel just a bit too big. But I loved 'em!'

Cortinas in motor racing

Although Cortina GTs were raced in 1963, the rest of the track story refers to Lotus-Cortinas, mostly with their Lotus-Ford twin-cam engines but sometimes, excitingly, with Cosworth-Ford FVA 16-valve F2 units.

Because the Lotus-Cortina was not homologated until September 1963, it could not be used in international saloon-car racing until then, so for the first season a team of Cortina GTs, run by John Willment, was pressed into service. Definitely 'works' instead of merely assisted – the Essex-based 'FOO ...' registration numbers gave the game away – they were always class winners, though they could never match the 7-litre Galaxies and Jaguar 3.8 Mk 2s at the front of the grids.

Even so, Jack Sears, Jimmy Blumer and Bob Olthoff were consistent class winners in the white-with-red striped Willment cars, so much so that Jack's car helped him to win the BRSCC British Saloon Car Championship outright, along with a Galaxie and a Lotus-Cortina! With eight class victories from eight starts, they were impeccably reliable – and only the Lotus-Cortinas, which then took over, were faster.

The same cars put up two fine long-distance performances in Europe, and there was one astonishing success in North America.

In the European Touring Car Challenge, Jack Sears/Bo Ljungfeldt won their class and finished third overall in the Brands Hatch Six Hours (behind two 3.8-litre Jaguars) while Sears on his own was winner of his class at Zandvoort.

The most famous victory of all, however, came in the Marlboro 12-Hour race in the USA, where the Willment cars finished first and second *overall*, beating everything that North American racing could throw at them. As Patrick McNally's end-of-season review in *Autosport* summarised:

'... the three Cortinas (two Willment and one Alan Andrews)

went like the devil between pit stops, these being many and varied. Jack Sears and Bob Olthoff (Willment Cortinas) won, despite various throttle linkage breakages and sundry other problems. The Andrews Cortina of Jimmy Blumer / Henry Taylor, which had led for much of the distance, dropped back to second, suffering from acute fuel starvation ...'

All these events, incidentally, were for FIA Group 2 cars – roughly equivalent to Group A in the 1990s, though in Group 2 more freedom was allowed to homologate special parts for engines.

Lotus-Cortina – an immediate winner in the UK

Once the A-frame/coil spring Lotus-Cortina made its appearance, it caused the sensation that Walter Hayes had always envisaged. Once again, to quote Paddy McNally:

'The Gold Cup meeting at Oulton Park [in September 1963] saw the first international debut of the recently homologated Lotus-Cortinas. Although not the outright winners, they were tremendously impressive, finishing third and fourth behind the Galaxies of Dan Gurney and Graham Hill.'

But this was just the start, for the Lotus-Cortinas were still only running with 145bhp. For 1964, not only would Team Lotus get the job of running a British Championship effort, but F1 drivers Jim Clark and Peter Arundell usually drove the cars. Because of their front-wheel-waving antics in the corners, BJH 417B, BJH 418B and BJH 419B became famous.

The season's story is easily told. Jim Clark started all eight rounds in the BRSCC series, won every class every time – and even threw in three outright victories as well. Nothing could be more emphatic than that. To quote McNally:

'The works Lotus-Cortinas were well prepared and exceedingly fast, proving capable of winning a race outright if the Ford Galaxies absented themselves for any reason.

'Initially these cars suffered from understeering characteristics induced, as much as anything, by the steering geometry, which might be criticised. But much development work was done in the steering department, and when fitted with thick anti-roll bars the cars were very rapid, even though their tendency to lift the front wheels made them unstable.'

They were, indeed, a whole lot more sophisticated than their more powerful rivals, much lighter than any of them, and with a great deal better balance and 'chuckability' – Jim Clark always making the most of this characteristic.

For 1965 the cars were even faster than before, because BRM took on the race-engine development contract – with a development team led by Mike Hall, who later moved to Cosworth – pushing up peak horsepower figures for the slightly overbored 1594cc units to about 150bhp at 7800rpm, and as soon as possible changing over to a conventional leaf-spring rear suspension. Jim Clark and Jack Sears drove the cars – JTW 496C, JTW 497C and JTW 498C.

This was the year in which John Willment's team cars were sometimes as competitive as the Team Lotus 'works' machines, and at the end of the year the cars were finally beaten by Roy Pierpoint's 4.7-litre Ford Mustang, but they were even faster than in 1964 and just as exciting to watch.

Lotus-Cortinas always won their 2-litre capacity class, with Jim Clark and Jack Sears winning three times each: Jim also won two events outright – once at Goodwood and once at Oulton Park.

For 1966 the scene changed considerably, for cars now had to run to FIA Group 5 regulations which gave almost unlimited freedom for mechanical change. The British Team Lotus cars – the PHK ... D team cars – therefore ran with wishbone front suspension, 180bhp

A happy man at work – Jim Clark three-wheeling his Team Lotus Lotus-Cortina race car through a Brands Hatch corner, the stance which thrilled so many race fans in the mid-1960s. Jim became British Saloon Car Champion in 1964.

fuel-injected BRM/Cosworth-tuned engines, and cast magnesium road wheels.

In a ten-event season, one or other of these cars won outright three times, and always won the 2-litre capacity class. Jim Clark and Peter Arundell drove the cars – Jim scoring all three race victories and five class wins – but so did Sir John Whitmore and Jacky Ickx. Chopping and changing drivers meant that none of them could win the Drivers' title, but Team Lotus lifted the Makes title. (The only cars which could beat them in a straight fight were 7.0-litre Galaxies and 4.7-litre Mustangs and Falcons.)

For 1967, Team Lotus elected to make yet another major change of direction. Not only did Ford decide that it should use the new-shape Lotus-Cortina Mk II, but a careful read of Group 5 regulations showed that it could be powered by the brand-new 16-valve Cosworth-Ford FVA Formula 2 power unit. This meant that the latest saloons would have 205bhp – very peaky, but undoubtedly effective!

After a tentative start to the year, when the upgraded 1966 Mk I cars had to be used, a new set of cars – CTC 12E/13E/14E – first appeared at the Silverstone meeting in April, where Lotus's new recruit, Graham Hill, was the driver. During the season Hill was joined by John Miles and Jacky Ickx, the main class opposition coming from Vic Elford's newly homologated Porsche 911.

Class wins, however, were one thing, but in 1967 not even the FVA-engined cars could compete with the 4.7-litre and 5.3-litre Fords (which were also taking every advantage of the Group 5 regulations). During the year, a 'works' Lotus-Cortina usually won its capacity class, but could never finish higher than third overall.

As with the rally programme, so with the racing programme. Ford knew that the new, and more promising, Escort Twin-Cam would be announced in January 1968, and that it intended to concentrate on those cars in future. Accordingly, after five flamboyant racing seasons, the official Lotus-Cortina racing programme was quietly laid to rest, and although the Frank Gardner/Alan Mann Racing team raced a red-and-gold Lotus-Cortina at the very start of the 1968 season, this was only a stopgap until the Escort Twin-Cams which Gardner made famous were ready for use.

A surprising number of these race cars seem to have survived.

Success in Europe, too

The 'works' Lotus-Cortina effort in Europe began in 1964, with Alan Mann Racing of Surrey running the team. Cars driven variously by Sir John Whitmore, Peter Procter, Peter Harper and Henry Taylor were always on the pace, but the opposition (from Alfa Romeo and BMW) was always intense.

Because of a weird points-scoring system, which favoured class wins rather than outright victory, the team was actually deprived of the title by BMC's much slower Mini-Cooper S models – even though the Lotus-Cortinas took six outright victories and five second places from eleven starts!

Sir John Whitmore, 'The Bearded Baronet,' as he was soon nicknamed, was outstanding in this team, taking five of those outright victories at events as far-flung as Brands Hatch, Austria, Switzerland and Belgium. All this, by the way, came from a car which still seemed to have much potential locked inside the engine, and in its first full year of racing.

The Alan Mann campaign in the 1965 European series was even more outstanding, for it was as near to a walkover as motor racing had seen for years. In a nine-event European Touring Car Championship season, with eight races and hill climbs concentrated into a three-month period, the red-and-gold Lotus-Cortinas were

The Lotus-Cortina was always a supremely successful race car. In 1964 BTW 297B was driven by Sir John Whitmore and Peter Procter to win the Six Hour International Saloon Car race at Brands Hatch.

Factory-backed Lotus-Cortina Mark IIs raced in 1967 and early in 1968, sometimes with Ford Cosworth FVA F2 engines. The scene is Silverstone in July, when Paul Hawkins's car won its capacity class.

always the class of the field. To quote Patrick McNally's end-of-season comment in *Autosport*:

'In the European Touring Car Challenge Sir John Whitmore was outstandingly successful, his Alan Mann Lotus Ford Cortina proving to be both fast and reliable. The popular racing baronet often won his races outright as well as the class, and shattered course and circuit records everywhere he went.

'Sir John Whitmore won not only because he had a well-prepared car and good team management, but because he simply out-drove the opposition.'

Although Sir John was not the only team member – other well-known personalities included Jack Sears and Peter Procter – he won three races and one hill climb outright, won his class in two other hill climbs, and was only beaten

twice. Even the defeats didn't matter all that much for he still won his class on both occasions, while the winning car was a Ford Mustang driven by the Norwegian Bo Ljungfeldt.

Ford was so proud of this achievement that it used the championship-winning car as a display vehicle for some time. The car was eventually acquired by Sir John in 1967 and he loaned it to the National Motor Museum at Beaulieu, where it stayed for some years.

At the very start of the season, Mann used the last of his 1964 cars, but this was only a stopgap. He already knew that the much-revised 'leaf-spring' Lotus-Cortina would be homologated in June – and since there was only one European event before then, he preferred to build cars for the new season to the latest spec.

Under serious cornering stress the cars would – as ever – roll considerably: the rear wheels would stay on the ground to keep transmitting power, but the inside front wheels would sometimes leave the ground completely. It looked wrong, though the drivers always insisted that they could feel nothing amiss. Whitmore and Jim Clark,

'Works' Lotus-Cortina performance

While I was working on *Autocar* magazine in 1967, I persuaded Ford to lend us a 'works' group Lotus-Cortina Mk II rally car for test – the actual car in which Ove Andersson and John Davenport had just won the gruelling Gulf London Rally.

The original colour scheme of this particular car – Saluki Bronze with Lotus Yellow stripe – was distinctive, but because it had also finished third in the Acropolis Rally – with Bengt Söderström as driver – and competed in the Swedish Jant event, UVW 924E was now looking distinctly careworn.

The body shell, Ford said, was now good only for scrap, and the car had not been rebuilt after the Gulf London Rally, but had been subjected to a quick wash only and removal of the competition numbers. Even so, Geoff Howard and I found nothing wrong with the performance! Ford Motorsport made no particular claims for the 1594cc engine's peak power output, though we reckoned it was about 140bhp. It looked remarkably standard to us, except that there was no air cleaner on the Weber carburettors.

Before checking out the performance, we had to remember that this was a heavy car, complete with extra stiffening, lamps, rally equipment, sump guards, etc. – we didn't have time to weigh it – and it was running on a back axle ratio of 4.70:1 (for rallies only).

First the figures, then the impressions:

Times in seconds	Works' Rally car	Standard Mk II
0-60mph	9.4	11.0
0-80mph	16.3	20.1
50-70mph in 3rd gear	5.4	6.9
50-70mph in top gear	7.5	12.4
70-90mph in top gear	8.7	18.7

The 'works' Cortina rally cars: major successes

GT models

1963

Acropolis	Henry Taylor/Brian Melia	4th
	Pat Moss/Ann Riley	6th
Midnight Sun	Bo Ljungfeldt/B.Rehnfeldt	3rd
Alpine rally	Henry Taylor/Brian Melia	3rd
	David Seigle-Morris/B. Hercock	4th
Spa-Sofia-Liège	Henry Taylor/Brian Melia	4th
	(using a Lotus twin-cam engine)	

1964

East African Safari	Peter Hughes/Bill Young	1st
	Mike Armstrong/Chris Bates	3rd
	Manufacturers' Team Prize	Winners
Tulip	Henry Taylor/Brian Melia	5th
Alpine	Vic Elford/David Stone	1st in Category
RAC	Vic Elford/David Stone	3rd
	Bengt Söderström/Bo Ohlsson	5th
	Manufacturers' Team Prize	Winners

1965

East African Safari	Vic Preston/George Syder	3rd
Circuit of Ireland	Vic Elford/David Stone	2nd
	Roger Clark/Jim Porter	3rd
	Brian Melia/Geoff Davies	4th
	Manufacturers' Team Prize	Winners
Shell 4000	Henry Taylor/Robin Edwardes	2nd

1967

East African Safari	Peter Hughes/R.Syder	3rd
	Jack Simonian/Peter Huth	6th
	Manufacturers' Team Prize	Winners

Lotus-Cortina

1963

RAC	Henry Taylor/Brian Melia	6th

1965

Alpine	Henry Taylor/Brian Melia	3rd in Touring Category
Welsh	Roger Clark/Graham Robson	1st

1966

Monte Carlo	Roger Clark/Brian Melia	4th (but disqualified)
	Bengt Söderström/Gunnar Palm	5th (but disqualified)
Flowers (Italy)	Vic Elford/John Davenport	1st (but disqualified)
Circuit of Ireland	Brian Melia/Geoff Davies	2nd
Tulip	Vic Elford/John Davenport	2nd
Acropolis	Bengt Söderström/Gunnar Palm	1st
	Roger Clark/Brian Melia	2nd
Vltava (Czech)	Bengt Söderström/Gunnar Palm	2nd
Tour de Corse	Henri Greder/H.Vigneron	5th
RAC	Bengt Söderström/Gunnar Palm	1st

1967

Swedish	Bengt Söderström/Gunnar Palm	1st
East African Safari	Vic Preston Junior/R.Gerrish	2nd
Acropolis	Bengt Söderström/Gunnar Palm	3rd
Gulf London	Ove Andersson/John Davenport	1st
1000 Lakes	Ove Andersson/Nordlund	4th
	Bengt Söderström/Gunnar Palm	5th
Three Cities	Bengt Söderström/Gunnar Palm	2nd

1968

Swedish	Bengt Söderström/Gunnar Palm	3rd
East African Safari	Peter Huth/Ian Grant	2nd

'Works' sponsored Cortinas in racing – Britain and Europe

Britain

1963
(Cortina GT)
BRSCC Saloon Car championship

	Jack Sears	4 Class wins
	Jimmy Blumer	2 Class wins
	Bob Olthoff	2 Class wins

Although the 4.70:1 axle limited top speed to a mere 97mph (at 7500rpm), with only 75mph available in third gear, these acceleration comparisons tell their own story:

At the same time, the fuel consumption was surprisingly good, at 23.3mpg overall.

As so often, these tell only part of the story. On the road, it was clear that this was an engine which needed to be kept singing above 4500rpm, or thereabouts. To quote Geoff Howard's text:

'It is possible to potter along at only 1800rpm, quite quietly at dead of night, but opening up from this speed causes a deep and vibrant growl, which suddenly switches to full noise from 4800rpm onwards. At 5600 all the torque comes in as well, and for really rapid progress the rev-counter must be kept swinging between 4500 and 7500rpm, which we took as the limit ...'

Let's be honest – we loved every minute of it. We loved the looks, which included Minilite alloy wheels and chunky all-weather Goodyears; we loved the handling, which was surprisingly subtle. And then:

'One thing was impressive above all else. The whole car felt extremely sensitive to the steering, almost nervous, so that there was no reaction delay at all before it changed direction, often before the driver was conscious of moving the steering wheel.

'Of the works cars we have now tested, this Ford is by far the most civilised and comfortable. It is certainly extremely exciting, and the kind of machine that one can never leave standing; it just has to be driven.'

If this car was good, and an international rally winner, what would it have been like to have driven one of the 180bhp fuel-injected race cars?

(Lotus-Cortina)		
BRSCC Saloon Car championship	Jack Sears	1 Class win
	Jim Clark	1 Class win
– all subsequent wins were in Lotus-Cortina		
1964		
BRSCC Saloon Car Championship	Jim Clark	3 Outright wins
		8 Class wins
		Championship win
1965		
BRSCC Saloon Car Championship	Jim Clark	2 Outright wins
	3 Class wins	
	Jack Sears	3 Class wins
1966		
BRSCC Saloon Car Championship Group Five	Jim Clark	3 Outright wins
		2 Class wins
	Other team drivers	5 other Class wins = championship
1967		
BRSCC Saloon Car Championship (Group 5)	Graham Hill/Paul Hawkins/Jacky Ickx	4 Class wins

Europe

1964		
European Touring Car championship	Sir John Whitmore	5 Outright wins
	Peter Procter (With Sir J. Whitmore)	1 Outright win
	Henry Taylor	1 Outright win
	Alan Mann Racing	2nd in, and class win in Championship
1965		
European Touring Car championship	Sir John Whitmore	4 Outright wins
		2 2nd places
		2 other Class wins
		Championship win

	Jack Sears (with Sir J. Whitmore)	1 Outright win
1966 European Touring Car championship	Sir John Whitmore	4 Outright wins

Other Countries

1963 (Cortina GT) Marlboro 12 Hour	Jack Sears/Bob Olthoff	1st
	Jimmy Blumer/ Henry Taylor	2nd

UVW 924E worked hard in mid-1967, finishing third in the Acropolis Rally; then – as seen here – used by Ove Andersson and John Davenport to win the Gulf London Rally.

The new and old styles at Silverstone in 1967 – Lucien Bianchi's Mark II Lotus-Cortina race car ahead of an ex-works 1966 example.

too, used these wheel-waving antics to get even tighter into the apex of a corner.

As a young Jackie Stewart is reputed to have commented about the cars:

'They're such a laugh, you can nae take them seriously!'

However, as Sir John himself once explained many years later:

'We built in a little bit of rear end steer to make it controllable, but in spite of its strange antics you can change line accurately; in a race you could dodge around in a corner quite well to get past some unexpected incident without losing too much speed.'

Even so, fame at this level is always brief. After its intense eight-event campaign in three months, KPU 392C was taken

back to England, given a cosmetic make-over by Ford and used in a dealership and Motor Show promotional tour. By 1966 it was beginning to look neglected, had lost much of its special equipment and went into storage.

The Championship-winning car never raced again, nor was the Lotus-Cortina ever as successful again on the track. But what a season!

For Alan Mann, the 1966 season was something of an anticlimax, for in Group 2 the 'works' Alfa Romeo GTAs had become extremely well homologated and very fast. Even so, the famous combination of Sir John Whitmore and these Lotus-Cortinas won four of the ten events outright (though two of them were speed hill climbs – at Mont Ventoux in France and Eigenthal in Switzerland).

This, though, was the end of Ford's official Lotus-Cortina programme in Europe. Not only had the ultra-specialised (and only marginally sporting-legal) Alfa Romeo GTA made the Lotus-Cortina obsolete, but the original-shape Lotus-Cortina had also dropped out of production and Ford did not think the heavier Mk II variety could be competitive.

All in all, the Hayes/Chapman vision of 1962 was turned triumphantly into fact. In the 1990s, the difficulty Ford has had in producing consistently successful Mondeo racecars has made many people look back to the Lotus-Cortinas:

'You did it then,' some cynics have said, 'so why can't you do it now?'

The 'GT' shield on the rear wings might be small, but there was nothing discreet about the Cortina GT's performance. With an engine tune influenced by Cosworth, this was a fast-selling 90mph-plus sports saloon.

From late 1964, this new fascia was part of the Cortina Mark I – the third in only two years. This one is a rarity, by British standards, with steering-column gearchange.

The 'facelift' for the Mark I was introduced in October 1964, and was more significant than it looked. This was the first Cortina to feature face-level ventilation, and it helped push sales on towards the second million.

These were the conditions the Cortina GTs had to survive to win the Safari in 1964 – and the mud was often much deeper than this!

A famous victory! The winning drivers, Peter Hughes and Bill Young, sitting on the roof of their Cortina GT, which has just won the 1964 Safari Rally. Boreham's organising team of managers, technicians and mechanics is grouped proudly round the car.

Ford made much of its entry in the 1964 East African Safari Rally. Before the event, the 'works' cars are lined up in front of a fleet of Kenyan Cortina demonstrator cars of the period.

Right from the start, the Cortina GT was a successful competition car – whether in races or rallies. The picture says it all – Ford draws attention to its success at the end of 1963.

The Lotus-Cortina of 1963-66 was the original Ford 'homologation special.' It was immediately successful on the race tracks and went on to win world-class rallies too.

Suitably prepared, the A-frame Lotus-Cortina was always a great race car. The Alan Mann cars led the Spa 24-Hour race for some considerable time in 1964, before transmission failure caused retirement.

By 1964 the 'works' Cortina GTs were formidable rally cars on loose or tarmac surfaces. Here we have Vic Elford/David Stone on the 1964 French Alpine.

Details denote the 1965 model's specification: CORTINA instead of CONSUL on the bonnet, full-width grille, air outlets in the rear quarters.

This Ford publicity shot of a 1967 model Mark II GT is so typical of the 1960s, and the chequered flag motifs signal success.

This 1969-model left-hand-drive 1600E fascia/instrument panel shows how far the Cortina's image had drifted upmarket since 1962. The 1600E customers – 58,000 of them – couldn't be wrong.

The 1600E of 1967-70 was for those GT enthusiasts who couldn't afford a Lotus-Cortina, but wanted to stand out from the crowd ... and so they did!

The 1600E arrived in 1967, with an upmarket image and high-spec trim and furnishings. The E was for Executive – as usual, Ford pitched its marketing exactly right.

The Mark II had a simple rear style, complete with wrap-around rear light clusters.

The Lotus-Cortina eventually became a great rally car. This picture shows Roger Clark and Jim Porter on their way to winning the Scottish in 1967 in a Mark II version.

Built at Dagenham, instead of by Lotus at Cheshunt, the second-generation Lotus-Cortina was still fast, but more civilised than before.

Although the Mark II used the same platform, suspension and running gear as the original Cortina, the body style was totally different. This is a 'facelift' 1600 Super of 1969.

Rostyle wheels, extra driving lamps, pin-stripes along the sides ... this could only be the 1600E of 1967-70.

Don't get too excited boys, she's wearing a wedding ring. This was the interior layout of the left-hand-drive 2000E of 1973-76.

The Mark III Cortina was the first to use the brand-new overhead-cam Pinto engine. In the GXL, the two-litre engine could push it up to more than 100mph. Quite an advance on 1962!

From almost every angle, the third-generation Cortina showed off some transatlantic Ford styling influence. This was the original Ford-Germany Taunus saloon, with different skin styling.

From 1973, there was also the Mark III 2000E, harking back to the 1600E for its heritage, complete with a well-trimmed interior and improved chassis. The new grille and rectangular headlamps were shared by other Cortinas from this point.

From this angle, the Mark III's 'coke-bottle' rear quarter styling looks very pronounced. The sports wheels were very popular on this and several other Ford models of the day, including Escorts and Capris.

When the Cortina Mark III was launched in 1970, Ford-Germany introduced closely related Taunus TC types, including this unique fastback coupé, which was never sold in the UK.

Compared to the Mark IV, the Mark V had deeper cabin windows all round, and much larger stop/tail/indicator lamps. It was in production from late 1979 to mid-1982.

From late 1976, the Cortina became the Mark IV, with this rather angular body style (which had been developed by Ford-Germany).

By the mid-1970s, Cortina interiors were much better and more completely trimmed than those of the original cars had ever been. This is a Mark IV GL of 1976.

Although the Ford-Germany 2.3-litre V6 was a wide engine, it fitted easily into the Mark IV's engine bay.

The badge tells its own story. From late 1977 the Cortina Mark IV was also available with a 2.3-litre V6 engine producing 108bhp.

The Mark IV shape was introduced in 1976, the British and German (Taunus) versions now looking identical. This shape would only last for three years before enjoying a serious 'facelift' for the final Mark V.

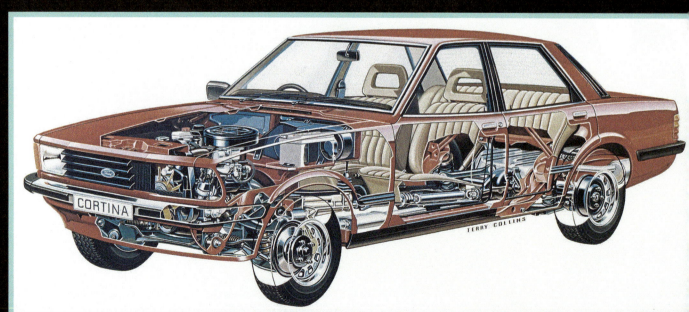

This was the architecture of the final Cortina – Cortina 80 or Cortina Mark V – showing the simple chassis layout which was so popular, and so successful, for so long.

Although the Mark IV shared its platform and running gear with the Mark III, the body style was simpler but more angular than before.

The very last British-built Cortina rolled off the lines at Dagenham in mid-1982. Ford-UK Chairman and Managing Director Sam Toy (in dark suit) help to celebrate. Before long the same lines would be full of Sierras.

This was how Ford promoted the Cortina's heritage when the Mark III appeared in 1970: three generations of Cortina matched to three generations of female fashion.

Another of Ford's favourite 'generations' themes at the launch of the Mark IV in 1976, with Mark I, Mark II and Mark III types in the background.

5

CORTINA III
THE TRANSATLANTIC
APPROACH

In many ways the Cortina of the next generation – the Mk III – could not have been more different from the model it was to replace. Technically it was almost all new, while the style was much more transatlantic than anything that had gone before. Except for the famous badge, there was very little to link the new with the old.

Although you might not be a great fan of the Mk III's style, you had to admit that it was very clever in detail. Although the car itself had a 3.5-inch longer wheelbase than before, and therefore a larger and more capacious cabin, it was exactly the same overall length as before. It might *look* much larger, but it was a mere two inches wider, and a full four inches lower, than the Mk II.

The word 'new' kept appearing in all the briefings, releases and descriptions – and there was every justification. Not only was there a new platform and style, but a new chassis layout and suspensions, a new overhead-camshaft engine and new transmissions. Not only that, but the Cortina had been pushed upmarket with a larger and more powerful two-litre engine at the top of the range.

It was high time that the Cortina platform was renewed: the original 98-inch wheelbase platform had lasted for eight years and two generations of Cortina, and in Ford terms this made it obsolete by almost any standards. We did not know it at the time, but the new platform would remain in production for twelve years.

Three generations of Cortina captured at the launch of the original Mark III. (The models are wearing clothes appropriate to the year in which each type was introduced.)

Ford-UK wanted the new Mk III to perform two rôles – to take over from the Mk II *and* from the larger Corsair, for that car was due to drop out of production before the new Mk III was ready.

An additional factor, which did not become clear until the first of the Granadas was introduced in 1972, was that it would be necessary for the larger car and the new Mk III Cortina to share some new chassis and suspension components because of soaring investment costs.

Most important of all, however, was that this would be the first range of Cortinas conceived under Ford-of-Europe, rather than under only Ford-UK control.

Ford-of-Europe – a new colossus

I must now spend at least a little time explaining why, and how, Ford-of-Europe came into existence in 1967.

Until the mid-1960s, Ford-UK had always competed, head-on, with Ford-of-Germany in world markets. In certain countries Ford-of-Germany dominated the market, with Ford-UK not even bothering to compete. In others – Holland was a perfect example – dealers often had both types of vehicle in their showrooms:

'This was part of the "two-fishing-line" approach,' Terry Beckett told me, 'where we were convinced that at that time this was

the way to get the best market share. It helped give them an additional spread of the market, and the reassurance that if one offering from one side or the other was a bit of a dog, they'd got something else!'

Over in the USA, for many years Henry Ford II had been too busy grappling with problems in Detroit to demand a shake-up of his European operations, but a Ford-International operation had been set up in 1959:

'That cried out for consolidation,' says Beckett, 'and Patrick Hennessy, in fact, always had a terrible time with John Bugas, an ex-FBI man, and a personal friend of Mr Ford, who was the Executive Vice-President of Ford-International, and a very powerful man.'

The change came in the mid-1960s when, according to Walter Hayes:

'Mr Ford started to push for consolidation. He was much more cosmopolitan than his American executives. He insisted that studies should be made on a proposal to set up Ford-of-Europe.'

At first the studies aroused great controversy, but then:

'Mr Ford called me, summoned me to the Plaza Athenée hotel in Paris. "John Andrews is coming from Ford-of-Germany, and so is Stan Gillen from Britain." I didn't know what was brewing, though.'

It was a very decisive meeting. Henry Ford II stated, baldly, that 'there has been too much farting

about on the whole business … ,' looked squarely at John Andrews, and told him:

'I'm going to make you President of Ford-of-Europe, so you'd better go away and work out how to make it work.'

Andrews, a tall rangy American who spoke fluent German, was hugely admired, and soon drew up his framework. Fortunately for Ford-of-Britain, there was lots of spare space in the brand new HQ office building at Warley, so Ford-of-Europe's centre of gravity settled in Essex, where it would remain until the early 1990s.

'Andrews realised, I think, realised early on that what we had to do was to build on our strengths. It was perfectly clear,' Walter Hayes states, 'that the UK was substantially superior in engines. There were aspects such as fit, finish, quality and bodies where the Germans were clearly superior. Ford-of-Germany had a wonderful test track at Lommel, which went on to become the European-wide test centre.

'For many there had to be a culture change – it's a pity this sort of thing was not done earlier. Eventually, of course, as co-ordination progressed, one could see how valuable it all was.'

Even before then, Ford-of-Germany had already got together with the UK to develop the 'Common Van' project – which became the Transit, a vehicle which has always

Testing of production-standard prototype Mk III Cortinas in Finland in 1970. The local-colour reindeer and sled just 'happened to be there' when the picture was taken.

Comparison of model dimensions		
Model	Wheelbase (in)	Length (in)
Cortina Mk II	98.0	168.0
Taunus 12M/15M	99.6	170.0
Corsair	101.0	176.8
Cortina Mk III	101.5	168.0

been built in two countries, always been the market leader, and which has now become a household name rather like 'Hoover' or 'Biro.'

The Ford-UK Escort launched in January 1968 also went into production in Germany at the end of the same year, but the first true Ford-of-Europe model, with simultaneous introduction in both countries, was the Capri – 'The Car You Always Promised Yourself.'

In 1967 and 1968, with the Capri well and truly under way, the new organisation could then turn its attention to a new medium-sized car. As far as the British customer was concerned, the result was the Cortina Mk III.

Cortina Mk III and Taunus TC – close relatives

By 1967 Ford-UK's business was booming while Ford-of-Germany was still struggling. The existing Cortina Mk II was Britain's best-seller, while the Corsair was selling well, if not sensationally. Ford-

Germany's equivalent was the V4-engined latest front-wheel-drive 12M/15M range, which was roughly equivalent to the Cortina.

In a very brave move, Ford-of-Europe decided to sweep all the old cars away and replace them with a single new project. The unsuccessful front-wheel-drive Taunus would be abandoned completely, and there was no need (no financial justification, either) for a replacement Corsair.

In Britain the new car would be the Cortina Mk III, and in Germany, with different styling but the same basic platform and inner structure, it would be a new-generation Taunus TC. To cover all the possibilities the new car had to have a longer wheelbase.

The TC acronym was widely used by everyone at Ford at the project and development stage (TC quite simply standing for Taunus Cortina). In every way, this was a European rather than a British project, for the entire car was drawn up around the metric system.

The new 'TC' cars were all to be based on the same platform, suspensions, front and rear tracks, and would have the same interior panels (such as the front bulkhead and windscreen pillars, inner front wings and some structure around the rear seat), plus the same roof panels. Beyond this, each company would be allowed to develop its own exterior style, and each would be able to choose a range of engines.

More experienced analysts than I have sometimes been hoodwinked by the American genius for making much difference from little change – and this was a classic case.

The cars would also have different names. Cortina was – and always would be – virtually an unknown name in Germany, whereas Taunus was a thoroughly domestic title.

Not only was this a brave attempt at technical rationalisation, it was also one which would not be diluted by the passage of time. Started in 1967, the new designs – Cortina Mk III and Taunus TC – were both ready for launch in the autumn of 1970. An amazing number of people never even realised that they were based on the same platform.

Compared with the new Cortina, the Taunus had an altogether more bulky and rather more anonymous style, while there was also a two-door fastback coupé version, for which there was never a Cortina equivalent. From 1972, when the new and entirely different Granada series took over from the old Zodiac Mk IV, one could see the same styling cues on the Granada as on the Taunus.

I don't think I am insulting the Cortina Mk III's style when I suggest that it really looks rather American, for certainly there were no similarities or carry-over themes from the Cortina Mk II. At the time, in fact, within Ford-of-

Making sure that the choice of front-end styles would fit the sheet metal: another studio shot taken in the late 1960s.

The third-generation Cortina looked larger and more transatlantic in style than the Mark II, yet it was no longer than before. The style, complete with the 'coke-bottle' shaping over the rear wheels, was definitely inspired by Ford-USA's latest designs.

In 1970 Ford released this detailed 'Terry Collins' cutaway drawing of the new-generation Cortina Mk III, showing the coil spring/wishbone front suspension and coil spring/live rear axle rear suspension ...

Europe there was still quite a lot of styling influence from Detroit. It is instructive to look back at the new 1970 and 1971 models which were coming out of Ford-Detroit – the Pinto and LTD among them – to pick up some of the same 'cues.'

It is also important to recall that when this model was being developed, Ford-UK's technical chief was Harley Copp, a robust American with very American ideas! Much of what went into the car – specifically the wishbone front suspension, and the sharing of a new engine with the Ford-USA Pinto model – was inspired by him. As far as I know, at this time MacPherson strut front suspension had never been used on Ford-USA vehicles.

The new car's style included two features extremely popular with all Detroit-influenced stylists of the period – the characteristic 'Coke bottle' bulge over the rear wheels, and the very pronounced sharp edges to the top and front of the front wings, which were punched well forward to surround the grille. [Look at the new-generation Vauxhall Victor of the same period, and notice that this GM-controlled company had adopted similar lines.]

The new fascia, frankly, was more American than the latest Ford-USA designs, and not at all to everyone's taste. Although the instruments were heavily cowled, the wood, where fitted, looked (and indeed was) distressingly artificial, while the layout looked bitty, with

... while three years later, at 'facelift' time, there was a modified version of the same artwork, showing the new rectangular-headlamp nose, the revamped interior and the latest sports wheels.

No computers in those days. In the late 1960s this was how styling modellers shaped the fascia/instrument board of the original Cortina Mk III.

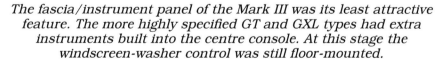

The fascia/instrument panel of the Mark III was its least attractive feature. The more highly specified GT and GXL types had extra instruments built into the centre console. At this stage the windscreen-washer control was still floor-mounted.

switches, dials and controls placed around rather haphazardly.

After the well-planned layout of the last Cortina Mk IIs, this was a great disappointment. Many observers thought the company could do better than this – and three years later it did.

New chassis engineering

Clearly this had been a hugely expensive new car to engineer, for – except for the Kent engine and its related gearbox – every chassis item hidden under the new style was new (and even the Kent engine had been updated).

The earlier cars' suspension and steering had all been swept away, for there was a new coil spring/wishbone front suspension (which the American-trained PR men insisted on calling SLA – short and long arm – suspension) along with rack-and-pinion steering, while at the rear there was a new Salisbury-type axle, complete with a malleable iron centre casting, while rear suspension was by coil springs, trailing and semi-trailing radius arms. [This type of rear suspension was extremely fashionable at the time: the Vauxhall Viva and, soon, the Hillman Avenger would all use the same layout. Incidentally, although it looked rather like the discredited Lotus-Cortina 'A-

This is one of a whole series of pictures showing what I believe was a pilot-build of an 'off-tools' Cortina Mk III in 1970. This type of front suspension was an entirely fresh layout for a European Ford.

Frame,' it was much better and more reliably detailed.]

Both existing Kent engines were uprated: the 1298cc unit to 57bhp and the 1599cc unit to 68bhp, but that was only a minor part of the story. The design of a brand-new overhead-camshaft engine, the 'Pinto' (see the panel on page 104) had been central to the new model's layout, this being available in 88bhp/1593cc or 98bhp/1993cc tunes.

Then and later the 'Pinto' was a controversial engine for it was taller and heavier than the Kent, not at all as reliable at first – there was quite a history of scuffed camshaft lobes caused by lubrication deficiencies – and not originally thought to be very tuneable. It was a very important Ford 'building block,' and would feature in every Cortina built between 1970 and '82.

Behind the two-litre engine, too, and new to Britain, there was

a four-speed all-synchromesh gearbox, a Taunus 20M variety with more torque capacity than the long-established British design, and one which would later be used in cars like the Escort Mk 2 RS models, some Capris and some Granadas.

> 2-door and 4-door saloons, plus a 5-door estate
> 1.3 and 1.6-litre Kent, 1.6 and 2.0-litre Pinto engines (57, 68, 88 and 98bhp)
> Base, L, XL, GT and GXL trim/equipment packs

A complicated line-up

Because of the many and various trim packs and options on offer, by any standards this was a complicated new range which I cannot possibly describe in detail! On announcement, there were no fewer than thirty-two different derivatives, permutated from the basics shown in the table.

In addition to these there was the option of automatic transmission, a colossal list of accessories (safety belts, tinted glass, radio fittings, and much more) and – just to confuse customers even further – no fewer than five different cross-ply and radial-ply tyre specifications on two different styles of pressed steel wheels, some of which were standard, some optional and some available only by special pleading!

The Cortina Mark III broke away from Ford-of-Britain tradition by using a coil spring/wishbone front suspension instead of the usual MacPherson strut layout. The anti-roll bar was only fitted to Pinto-engined cars at first, but was standardised across the range from the 'facelift' in autumn 1973. The Granada family, built from 1972 to 1985, used the same basic suspension, mounted to a different cross-member.

There was also a 1.1-litre Kent-engined car for some export markets, and a pick-up (the Australians would have called it a 'Ute' for Utility) was also developed but never sold in the UK.

Because Ford was now concentrating all its sporting efforts on Capris and Escort RS models, there was no place for a twin-cam-engined model, and nothing with a Lotus badge. Even though there was a 'GT' model in the new line-up, it neither felt nor looked as special as before.

In any case, by previous Cortina standards the new two-litre-engined model was much faster than earlier cars. This time the top speed was 105mph; 0-60mph acceleration took only 10.7 seconds, and (if it was built properly) this was a very satisfying machine. A 2000GXL was as fast as the obsolete Lotus-Cortina Mk II, so no-one was complaining.

Prices at launch started at £914 (1300 Base, two-door) through £1095 (1600XL, four-door) and all the way to £1338 (2000GXL, four-door). What can Ford have been thinking of? This made life almost impossible for the dealers.

I have personal knowledge of this, because when I changed jobs at the end of 1971, my 'business car' allowance would have been enough for me to specify a top-of-the-range Cortina, which in fact I wanted; yet getting hold of a car was a depressing experience.

To match the new Pinto engine, Ford-of-Europe also developed this new-style, all-synchromesh four-speed gearbox. In later years this box would eventually 'grow up' to have five forward speeds, and to be used in cars like the Sierra and the Capri 2.8 Injection models.

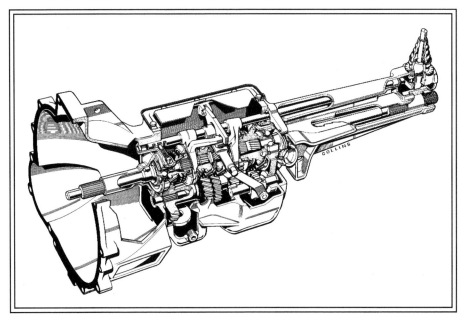

After wading through the catalogue, deciding that I wanted a 2000GT two-door in a particular colour, with certain extras, I then went along to my nearest Ford dealer to order the car. I won't say that the salesman laughed in my face, but he made it clear that I would have to wait for more than three months before something close to that specification could be built.

I admit that at this point I actually did laugh in **his** face, abandoned my good intentions and ordered a Triumph Dolomite 1850. And enjoyed it, by the way ...

Problems, problems

Just as the Mk III was ready for launch, fate stepped in. Pay talks collapsed, the workforce walked out, and Dagenham then had to suffer a nine-week strike during which no cars were built:

'We went to Eindhoven in Holland for a joint press launch with the Germans,' Harry Calton remembers, 'but we had a lot of supply problems. As the press launch went on, the number of Cortinas we had for the press to drive gradually increased.

'The common approach worked well, though. When we were in the middle of the launch, and needing some parts, I remember going to Genk [Belgium – the Taunus assembly plant] to collect them.

'But we were lucky. The cars that we had for the press launch were not exactly prime examples.

When the Cortina Mark III was introduced in 1970, there were two different noses – the four-headlamp nose being standard on GT and GXL types.

If we'd had a trouble-free launch, without that very long strike, and we had made the numbers of motor cars that we could have done at the time, then we might have had serious quality problems.

'The early cars were disastrous – the interior door handles were snapping off, the new Pinto engine was drinking oil because that was running down the valves, there were poor door fits, there were lots of other things ...

'Bill Hayden, a formidable manager but not a likeable man (he could be extremely abrasive and rude) was Director of Manufacturing and got everything sorted out. That long gap caused by the strike was our salvation, because the cars we then delivered to customers were considerably better built than the cars we had at launch.

'Virtually all those cars we used at the launch were scrapped – none of them was ever released on the retail market. *Tomorrow's World*, by the way, once used a TV sequence of

Pinto – the engine project

Ford-USA started planning for a new family of small cars (small, that is, by North American standards) in the late 1960s, finally introducing the new Pinto range in 1970. This was Dearborn's smallest car yet, and was originally offered with a choice of two four-cylinder engines – a British 'Kent' 1.6-litre and a brand-new 2-litre overhead-cam 'Pinto.'

Right from the start, the overhead-cam, five-main-bearing 'Pinto' was seen as a 'world' design, intended for use in many different new models. Rather tall and slender, it featured a cylinder-head layout new to Ford, with an overhead camshaft driven by a cogged belt. Two valves per cylinder were opposed at an included angle of 15 degrees, each being driven from the camshaft via steel fingers. Unlike the 'Kent,' it had conventional head-positioned combustion chambers, and used flat-top pistons.

Although it was originally manufactured by Ford-of-Europe in Cologne, the new engine was also supplied to Detroit for use in the Pinto car, and it was immediately on offer in the 1971-model Ford-Germany Taunus TC, and in the Cortina Mk III.

In European guise, it was originally built in 1294cc, 1593cc and 1993cc forms, and would go on to power many more Fords until the late 1980s, when it was replaced by a new twin-overhead-cam I4 2-litre. Other Pinto users included the Escort RS Mexico and RS2000, the Capri, the Granada and the Transit Van ... the engine was built in its millions.

Engine deliveries to the USA ceased in 1974 ('Kent' deliveries had ended in 1973) for this was the point at which the closely related Ford-USA 'Lima' engine (really an enlarged, 2301cc 'Pinto') took over completely for Ford-USA models, this new engine being built in Lima, Ohio, USA.

In the USA the 'Lima' family of engines was even more successful than the 'Pinto' on which it was based, being built until the mid-1990s into a variety of compact Fords, including the evergreen Mustang.

The Pinto engine, introduced by Ford in 1970 and used on several Cortina Mark III models, had a single overhead camshaft, belt-driven, with rockers to each line of valves.

The Pinto overhead camshaft engine was brand new in 1970, not only for use in the Cortina Mark III, but also in the USA-built Pinto model. This was the exhaust side of the unit ...

... and this was the inlet side, complete with twin-choke Weber carburettor in this two-litre 98bhp tune.

The Pinto engine featured this unique cylinder head and combustion chamber layout.

a car coming together – an explosion run backwards on film – which was one of those press cars. It was a very good way of getting rid of the damned thing ...'

Even so, Ford's planners knew that they *had* to get the car right, as its basic engineering and layout was due to take the Cortina range through – and beyond – the 1970s. Every effort was thrown into sorting out Dagenham, the suppliers (whose parts were slipshod at times) and, of course, the dealers, encouraging them to do their best.

This was the point at which the complication of the range reached new and lunatic heights. In fleet terms, the directors were allocated Granadas, managers got top-of-the-line Cortina GXLs, those below them were treated to XLs, the heavy-mileage 'on the road' reps got L-spec models – and then there were extra gradations which prompted Ford to extend its accessories list even further. Was there a market, for instance, for sunroofs ... leather trim ... heated rear windows ... tinted glass?

All of this and more was imposed on Dagenham, and on the long-suffering dealers. By the early 1970s, the entire range was so alarmingly complicated that slow-selling versions soon had to be deleted. Two-litre Base, two-door L and estate cars disappeared in 1972, 1.3-litre XLs followed suit, and there were no 1.3-litre-engined estates by 1973. Two-door GXLs

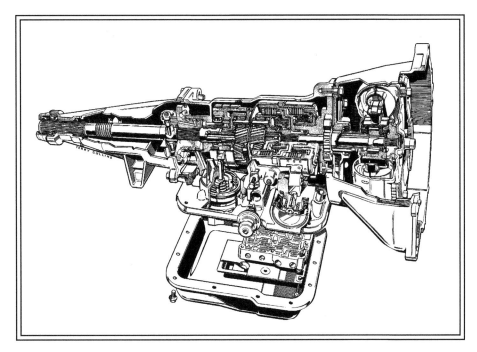

Earlier Cortinas used Borg Warner automatic transmission, but from the early 1970s the company introduced its own brand of C3 automatic box instead, which was built at a new factory near Bordeaux, France. During the 1980s this box of tricks would be upgraded to have four forward ratios.

and two-door GTs followed during 1973, and by this process the range was reduced in 1973 to a more manageable, but still massive, twenty derivatives!

Along the way the Cortina had become the archetypal 'rep car' or 'fleet model,' for there seemed to be a derivative, with the appropriate trim level, for every management grade:

'We'd started with a Base and a de Luxe,' Terry Beckett reminded me, 'then we went on to Super, then to GT. In the early days the accepted wisdom was that there wasn't a way you could extend the Cortina price range by more than 25 per cent. But we discovered, to my surprise, that by adding extra features we were able, in that price bracket, to go up by nearly 80 per cent over the price of the Base car.

'I think that by the 1970s Manufacturing had come round to the view that the market was getting more competitive, and they'd got to cope.'

Sam Toy, his successor as Ford-UK's Chairman, agrees with this:

'A great percentage of Cortina sales went to the fleets, and it became *the* rep's car. We also had a big chunk of the car hire market – in those days we got the biggest share of Hertz, Avis, Budget and Godfrey Davis.'

For all these reasons – and more – it wasn't easy to make the pundits excited about the new range. There was no longer a Lotus version to add stardust to the image, and – except for odd-ball uses in motor racing by publicity-conscious characters like Radio 1 DJ Noel Edmonds – Cortinas were no longer seen in motorsport.

Ford's PR advisers were careful to loan out the faster and better-equipped versions at first, which explains why *Autocar* tested a 2000GXL in the week of launch – loving everything about the performance and the handling, if not the equipment and build quality – and a more representative two-door 1600GT in the summer of 1971.

Even so, Geoff Howard and his team were distinctly sniffy about the 1600GT:

'The troubles which afflicted Ford in the early part of this year are too well known to need any reminder here ... Compared with the old Cortina 1600E, the new 1600GT is marginally slower all the way along the line. It has a little more power, but on the other hand its kerb weight is well over a hundredweight [50kg] more ... At the top end, its extra frontal area must also have some effect ... The 1600GT was distinctly disappointing where the ride was concerned ...'

On the other hand:

'The 1600GT gave us no cause to modify the very high opinion we formed of the 2000's handling. It could be safely cornered at very high speeds, well above average for a car in this class ... it understeers, gently at first, then increasingly strongly. At its limit, the front end ploughs straight on ... in many ways the Cortina 1600GT has a convincing set of virtues for the price.'

A mid-term facelift – and a new 2000E

By 1973 experienced Ford-watchers were beginning to expect changes to the Cortina range – after all, both the Mk I and Mk II versions had received facelifts after only two years. For the MK III, the 'freshener' finally came in September 1973.

Subtly but definitely, this was the point at which Ford began to move the marketing focus of the Mk III, moving it slightly upmarket, and shedding some visual Americanisms. Visually this was done in two days, by providing a new nose for the more expensive

From autumn 1973, the front-end style of upmarket Cortina Mark IIIs was changed, with new grilles, and with rectangular headlamps taking over from the original four-round-headlamp style. As before, two-door or four-door saloons were available.

types, a much smarter and very 'British' type of fascia/instrument panel for all types, and by launching a new top-of-the-range 2000E.

It was, however, not as simple as that – this was Ford, after all! At the same time as the facelift, there was a new engine line-up, new gearbox ratios for smaller-engined models, changes to the suspension settings and a revised interior.

Externally, there was little change for base and L models, but other types – XL, GT and the new 2000E – were given a new nose, complete with rectangular headlamps and quartz-halogen bulbs. (The original Mk III nose with its four circle headlamps disappeared at this point, probably to save money, though this was never admitted.)

Internally, the rather horrid original fascia (so American in its character and layout, and with such unlikeable switches and detailing) was dumped in favour of a smart new design. Only the inverted vee-spoke steering wheel remained from the old layout; as ever, the wheel was not quite circular, designed to give more space above the driver's legs.

Rectangular and all-of-a-piece rather than sinuous, with clear, well-positioned controls, this really was the smartest fascia Ford-of-

Europe had yet evolved for its cars. Surprisingly, the windscreen wipe/wash control was still a floor-mounted button, close to the clutch pedal on right-hand-drive cars.

Matching it for all versions was a totally re-worked ventilation system, a reversion to swivelling eyeball controls for face-level ventilation, a larger glovebox and, for the new 2000E, a neat centre console surrounding the gearlever and clock.

Although the familiar 1300-1600-2000 engine line-up was retained for 1974, the old 1.6-litre 'Kent' engine had disappeared, to be replaced by a 1.6-litre version of the overhead-cam 'Pinto.' With 72bhp instead of the old engine's 68bhp, this brought only a minor performance change – but it showed the way that Ford's long-term engine sourcing strategy was tending.

When it came to gearbox usage, however, Ford-of-Europe still seemed to be in disarray, for the company was still using no fewer than six different basic designs for its private cars. For 1974, at least, the internal ratios of 1300/1600 Cortina types were reshuffled to get rid of the large gap between second and third gears – this was overdue, for over the years there had been many complaints. For the record, the internal ratios of the latest cars

were stacked up as per the table on page 107.

Once again the chassis engineers had been allowed to tinker with the suspension, and although there were no basic changes to the layout or the geometry, front and rear settings had all been re-worked.

At the front, the original GT-only setup was adopted, which is to say that there was now to be an anti-roll bar for all models. All cars except the 2000GT were to use 73lb/in front springs, the GT getting much stiffer 106lb/in springs instead.

At the rear, too, there was to be a new anti-roll bar for all versions. All but the GT used 123lb/in coil springs, whereas the GT was fitted with 140lb/in coils instead.

Ford claimed that the overall effect was less roll, better balanced handling, a reduction in understeer and a better all-round ride. The GT, but *not* the other 2000-engined cars (especially the 2000E) had a much firmer and more sporting setup than before.

Ford hoped that the 2000E would be as appealing a package as the old 1600E had been, for that was a car which had repaid its meagre investment handsomely. There's no doubt that the latest car was inspired by the 1600E – if only because of the way that Ford kept on referring to it in display ads:

'It is without doubt the best Cortina we've ever built. It has even more class. It is even more

Internal gear ratios (1974)

Ratio	Early Mk III 1300/1600	Latest Mk III 1300/1600	2000 (no change)
Top	1.00	1.00	1.00
3rd	1.41	1.40	1.37
2nd	2.41	2.01	1.97
1st	3.54	3.58	3.65
Reverse	3.96	3.32	3.66

The smart and very well-equipped interior of the 2000E, complete with brand-new fascia/instrument panel and wood cappings. Note that this car also has the optional automatic transmission.

This two-door Mark III is a 1974 model, with the latest nose and the sports road wheels. The badges on the front wings tell us that it is a 2000GT.

Smile please! Ford went to great lengths to emphasise the luxury aspect of the 2000E. This is the automatic-transmission version.

restrained. 1600E owners, you have a new idol.'

Neither should we forget that the Cortina Mk III had also displaced the

The 2000E of 1973-76 was the best-equipped of all Mark III Cortinas, and was sold in saloon and estate car version (pictured here).

last of the sharp-nosed Corsairs, of which the Corsair 2000E had been a popular and successful derivative. Yet there had been no equivalent new version of the Cortina Mk II at first, this being another reason why a new top-of-the-range type was justified.

Like the old-style 1600E, the new 2000E was no more than a tasteful and thorough make-over of an existing type: looking back, it is easy to say that the harder GT-specification suspension should have been adopted – just as the 1600E had used Lotus-Cortina suspension settings at first – but these were the days when Ford was emphasising the comfort of the Cortina, not its sporting pretensions, and as far as I know this was never considered.

When evolving the 2000E package, Ford set out to develop a new Cortina flagship, including the best possible trim, furnishing and equipment in a two-litre Pinto-engined chassis. Looking back at what had sold so well in the 1600E, Ford offered more of the same, but with two major additions – Borg Warner automatic transmission was optional, and an estate car version was to follow one year later.

On the outside of the 2000E there was a vinyl roof as standard (still an optional extra on all other Mk IIIs) and rubbing strips along the flanks, with the usual highly

The Australian Cortinas

For more than ten years – 1972 to 1983 – Ford-Australia built a particular Cortina derivative which was never seen in Europe. Some components were supplied from Europe, but as year followed year, there was more local manufacture. Faster and heavier than any European type, these cars used big, lazy and torquey straight-six cylinder engines.

The first time I ever looked around one of these cars, it all seemed very familiar, and had nothing more exciting than a big '6' in chrome on the boot lid. Opening up the bonnet, however, brought a real surprise – for there, filling the engine bay completely, was a big straight-six cylinder engine. Not, you understand, the short and stubby vee-6 which we have all seen in European-style 1970s Cortinas, but a long, and obviously heavy straight-six. There was a big air cleaner box to hide some of the details, but what seemed to fill up all the space, and even keep out the daylight, was a veritable symphony in cast iron.

In the 1970s Ford-Australia liked to hedge its bets. Although the typical Australian car, by postwar tradition, was big and roomy for making those long journeys in the outback, millions of Aussies who lived closer to the big cities wanted something smaller.

The big cars – American-inspired Falcons, mainly – got progressively more and more Australian, but from 1972 to 1983 the alternative range was British-type Cortinas. Two years after the Cortina Mk III had gone on sale in Europe, Ford-Australia put it into production on the outskirts of Melbourne.

However, the range had a completely different balance. Instead of a jumble of small 'fours' and a vee-6, Ford-Australia Cortinas used only two-litre overhead-cam Pintos – or a choice of massive, heavy, in-line six-cylinder units (3.3 or 4.1 litres). Many of these 'sixes,' by the way, drove through Borg Warner automatic transmission.

Here was a car halfway to being what Australian drivers wanted ... or so the planners thought. The car itself was European in size, but the engine was lifted straight out of the Falcon, which had come across the Pacific Ocean ten years earlier from Detroit. Nine inches longer and two inches taller than the Pinto, the big 'six' would just – and only just – fit under the bonnet. To look after those long journeys, not only did the Falcon's engine have a massively beefy torque curve, but the axle ratio of the 4.1-litre car was raised to a colossally high 2.76:1. No European Cortina was ever as high-geared as this, nor any so easy to drive.

These straight-six engined Cortinas for Australia only were built for ten years in styles identical to our own Mk III, Mk IV and Mk V types. In all cases, the old-style Falcon engine was a top-of-the-range option – the 4.1-litre machine being seriously quick.

New-model pamphlets at the time urged: 'Drive it ... it makes beautiful sense ... When you choose a Cortina 6, you get the smooth, easy power of the 3.3-litre engine as standard, or, if you want real performance, you can order the optional 4.1-litre engine at extra cost ...'

The pictures show that there is really 'standing-room only' under the bonnet, and, in any case, the panel needed a hump of extra depth to give clearance over the air-cleaner. The original release admits that: 'the firewall panel [bulkhead] and plenum panel are new to allow for the longer six-cylinder engine and larger transmission housing. Similarly the floor pan ... has been modified to cater for the slightly increased width of the six-cylinder transmission.'

There was more. Different front springs and dampers were specified, while the front anti-roll bar was reshaped to clear the sump. The radiator had to be moved forward by three inches, the radiator itself needing to be wider and lower than the standard type, and there was a new structural member surrounding this.

The engine cross-member was extensively modified, not only by additional welding, but by using different gauge material. Engine mounting brackets had extra gussets, and there was an additional bolt-on body cross-member under the transmission. Matching this engine, the transmissions – manual or automatic – were from the Falcon, as was the rear axle.

polished sports road wheels. Based on the latest interior package, with the most fully equipped version of the brand-new instrument panel/fascia, there were also deep-pile carpets, real teak wood cappings for the fascia panel and waist-level door sills, plus a new type of Savannah nylon-cloth seat/door panel trim, a centre console and clock and push-button radio, all as standard.

Britain's inflation spiral – prices going up fast

Britain was suffering rapidly soaring inflation at this time, which would hit 16 per cent during the year, rocket to 24 per cent in 1974 and be followed by a further 24 per cent in 1975. Therefore I will quote 1974-model Cortina prices before they inflated out of all proportion.

At this stage there were fourteen different saloon types and four estates on offer (the 2000E estate would not be launched for a further year). Several two-door types remained, though their popularity was falling away, and representative prices of the four-door saloons were as per the table.

Even at this stage, incidentally, Ford was still charging an extra £17.05 for a pair of inertia-reel front seat belts. Although these had to be fitted by law to UK-market

Four door saloon prices (1974)	
1300	£1114
1300L	£1165
1600L	£1230
1600XL	£1350
2000XL	£1403
2000GT	£1437
2000E	£1638

machines, wearing them was not yet compulsory – and like other car manufacturers, Ford chose this way of pointing out the stupidities of the law as it stood.

The horrifying thing about British inflation in the mid-1970s was that all these prices would virtually double before the new Mk IV took over in the autumn of 1976, only three years later. At one stage prices were rising by six to eight per cent *every three months* in what looked like an unstoppable spiral. The whirlwind abated in the late 1970s, thank heavens, but those of us who were around at the time will never forget it.

Like almost every other section of the press, *Autocar* testers were impressed, but not overwhelmed, by the new 2000E. Although Ford had tried hard to replicate the character of the 1600E, this new model was not quite as startlingly different as its predecessor:

'Ford are to be congratulated,' the test summary stated, 'on providing a new model at the top of their Cortina range which does not really cost any more than the old GXL. With all its equipment and particularly luxurious interior, the 2000E has lots of appeal. It rides a little better than before, handles a lot better and is noticeably quieter. If they could only eliminate those last traces of harshness and boom, it would rate as a class leader on every count. As it stands, it is still a great car, typical of Ford's value

for money, and well deserving of its enormous sales success.'

This, incidentally, was a 98bhp car which achieved 102mph flat out, 0-60mph in only 10.6 sec, and was good for day-to-day fuel economy at around 27mpg.

Even so, by no means everything in the 2000E was standard equipment. As already pointed out, the compulsory seat belts were £17.05 extra, while a laminated screen cost £28.78, metallic paintwork £8.17 and larger-section (185/70) tyres a further £22.74. The on-the-road cost of the *Autocar* road test vehicle was £1745.

Autocar testers also stressed the marketing problems which the earlier Cortinas had needed to overcome:

'To recap briefly, the Mk III Cortina was introduced three years ago and immediately suffered some teething troubles, mostly caused by labour problems at the time of the launch ... Eager to stay on top, Ford went ahead with a revision programme, based on initial press and public criticism, which they have implemented for the 1974 Model year.'

The latest suspension package came in for detailed comment:

'Overall, the changes to the suspension have improved the car, the ride being more absorbent most of the time and pitch being better damped. At low speed, however, there is still a tendency for the rear

end to feel lively, and back-seat passengers commented several times on the unfamiliar motion, as if suspension movements were causing lateral reactions on the body.' [This was almost certainly due to the trailing/semi-trailing arm rear axle location, to which there was no solution without completely altering the geometry]

'Roll is naturally much reduced, and the 2000E corners with flat and very secure-feeling attitudes. It is a much better-balanced car now, without the ultimate straight-on characteristic and a kind of on-rails feel to the back end which always seems to follow round on line. In the wet, when it is surprisingly hard to break traction, the car behaves extremely well and very seldom flicks its tail out even a foot ... If this seems to be at variance with the new 1600XL, the difference lies in the power available and the way it can be fed to the wheels in a turn.

'Whatever the finer points of the handling, all Cortina drivers will notice the greater precision on the road and the way the new model can be driven with more confidence.'

The most important comment of all followed later:

'Inside and out, the standard of finish on the test car was something to admire. The metallic copper-bronze paint was well applied and the new and very luxurious deep-pile carpets were most impressive. In equally good taste were the matt teak cappings on fascia and doors.

109

Cortina 6 driving impressions – not like our Cortinas

On a visit to Australia in 1995, long-time owner Len Roser showed me his own Mk IV-style car, which had already completed 174,000km (108,000 miles) in his hands since he bought it new in 1979.

As soon as I started moving, I commented on the heavy steering. There is no power assistance on this car – nor could you get it, at any price, on Cortina 6s. Nowadays, of course, we're so used to power steering even on Fiestas, that you can guess what a shock it was to me.

This, and the 'moon-shot' acceleration, made me dive for a note which Ford-Australia sent me in 1989 when I enquired about this car. As Communications Manager Adrian Ryan wrote at the time:

'The six wasn't the greatest success story for Ford-Australia. The cars didn't handle all that well, due to the extra weight up front. They did accelerate like a racing car though!'

So I wasn't getting it all wrong – all Cortina 6s handled like this one. Well, with an American-style six-cylinder engine (which you also found in Fairlanes and Mustangs in the early 1960s) and with fat 205/65-13in tyres on 5.5in rim wheels, they would, wouldn't they?'

On the other hand, the torque – there was enough sheer low-speed grunt for this machine to scale Ayers Rock – was colossal, power delivery was seamless (if you didn't try to rev the old-style engine too high) and, with that very high gearing it would have been easy to repeat those transcontinental journeys Len Roser had tackled when the car was young.

It was hard work to lug the car round corners in suburban Melbourne, but it moved effortlessly in a straight line, and was not about to be pushed sideways by strong winds. Put your foot down from a red light and you got the same sort of rumble we all hear from a big 'Essex' – but this was a perfectly balanced 'big six' and the noise was somehow different. With Detroit iron throbbing up front, and a rev counter reading amazingly low (only 2000rpm in top gear at 80kph – 50mph), I was often tempted to go well over the speed limits, so ruthlessly enforced in Victoria.

In some ways it reminded me of a three-litre Capri, but when I mentioned that, neither Len nor anyone in the Australian RS Owners Club knew anything about those! Fascinating, but frustrating. Why was the European Cortina never as effortless as this? The 'Big Six' engine – an amazingly long life.

The six-cylinder engine in this Australian 'Big Six' Cortina has an amazingly long life-story to tell. Originally it started life as a USA-designed 101bhp/3.5-litre iron-head pushrod design, first seen in the 1952-model American Fords, and thereafter featured in the Falcons which were sent to Australia in the early 1960s.

The 3.3-litre/200CID and 4.1-litre/250CID engines used in these Cortinas were originally seen, in the USA, in the 1963 USA Fairlane and 1968 Mustang models respectively. This 'Detroit Iron' then featured in millions of Detroit Fords until, much modified, it was last used in an American Ford in 1983.

When Ford-Australia came to manufacture its own engines, this rugged 'six' was an obvious choice, and was used in the original 'all-Australian' Falcon XA of 1972.

Colour-keying of all the different interior trim materials was well executed, there were no unsightly gaps, and the moulded carpets were a perfect fit.'

Only a few weeks earlier, the same testers had tried the 1974-model 1600XL, noting all the changes, including the use of a rev-counter instead of a clock in the new fascia, generally liking what they found in the revised handling and equipment, and ending by stating that:

'For a host of reasons, the Cortina 1600XL has been Britain's top selling model in spite of some failings. Now that most of the weak points have been eliminated, especially by the provision of much better ventilation, it must surely do better still.'

Once again this test showed just how easy it was for a customer to bump up the so-called 'windscreen sticker price' of a Cortina Mk III. According to the lists, in September 1973 the retail price of a 1600XL was £1350, but the test car came in at £1525 – £175 or 13 per cent higher. Not only was this because of the price of seat belts, a road fund licence and number plates, but because the push-button radio, cloth upholstery, 5½J sports wheels, a brake servo, a laminated windscreen and metallic paintwork, which were all fitted, were all optional extras

Mk III¹/2: a three-year career

This time there were no delivery hiccups after the launch for Ford was ready to sell cars in great numbers. For the first few weeks, in fact, the British market was buoyant as ever. Then the 'energy crisis' bit hard, and deeply: there was the threat of petrol rationing, so-called 'temporary' speed limits followed and, to cap it all, the second and very bitter miners' strike paralysed the country in the early weeks of 1974.

Thereafter, and with the British economy seemingly in permanent crisis, the latest version of the Mk III had to struggle for every sale. Ford, however, reacted to all these traumas better than any of its British rivals (particularly British Leyland, which steadily lost market share) and it was two Ford models, the Cortina Mk III and the restyled Escort, which did so much to keep the company at the head of the lists.

Value for money additions

Base models:	**Brake servo**
	Hazard warning flashers
	Heated rear window
	Cloth seats
	Carpets
	Cigarette lighter
L models:	**All 'Base' additions plus:**
	Driver's door mirror
	Lockable glovebox
	Estate car rear wash-wipe
	Opening rear quarter windows (2-door)

XL models:	**All 'L' model additions plus:**
	Wheel trims
	Wooden instrument surround
	Clock/centre console
	Inertia reel seat belts
GT models:	**All 'XL' model additions**

The records show that the Cortina Mk III was Britain's best-selling car at this time – in 1972, 1973, 1974 and 1975.

In that first traumatic year, one major Cortina change went almost unnoticed: the optional Borg Warner Type 35 automatic transmission was finally dropped in favour of the new Ford C3 automatic transmission, which was now in full production at the Bordeaux factory.

These transmissions, incidentally, had been phased into the Ford-of-Europe range with almost no fuss at all, and also become optional on other British Fords – Capri II and Consul/ Granada types – at this time. In a much developed form, and later with four forward speeds, the transmissions would be fitted to all such front-engine/rear-drive European Fords built until the end of the twentieth century.

There was real stability in the Cortina range for the next two years, the only exceptions being the arrival of the 2000E Estate car in the autumn of 1974, and specification improvements to the 2000GT in January 1975. (New front seats with headrests, cloth upholstery, extra driving lamps and 185HR70-13-section tyres were all added.)

Then, in October 1975, it was

upheaval time again. The company introduced major specification changes for all its larger cars: Cortina, Capri and Consul/ Granada. These were in reaction to Britain's raging inflation, and to a slump in British car sales – British car production had dropped from 1.7 million to 1.2 million in two years, the British market having contracted by almost exactly the same amount.

This move was not entirely premeditated:

'By 1975,' Sam Toy recalls, 'our market was right down, to less than 20 per cent. Then, one night, I was sitting down to dinner with one of Bill Bourke's colleagues, who suddenly said: "How many of you fellows have got into a Cortina 1600L recently? It's as bare as a bird's arse – you've been taking costs out of that car so consistently that you are left with a nothing-product."....'

Knowing that the new-style Mk IV car was still almost two years away, Toy reacted very quickly. Although it claimed it could do little about rising prices, Ford stated that it would be 'giving away' £14 million worth of additional value for the 1976 model year. This, in a way, was a product planner's nightmare, for it had meant upgrading every model and re-specifying every version. Apart from retouching

the styling (such as a new black grille on all cars) the Cortina L, for example, now got a driver's door mirror, cloth seats, a brake servo, a locking glovebox and (on two-door cars) opening rear quarter windows as standard, while all estate cars were also given a rear wipe-wash installation.

How the VFM (value for money) additions stacked up can be seen in the above table.

By this time Cortina prices started at £1599 and reached £2690 – the first of the 1976-model 2000E saloons, for instance, was ticketed at £2456.

Accent on economy

Although the energy crisis of 1973-74 had terrified the world's motor industry, it took time to develop the 'economy' models which dealers and customers immediately requested. Starting from scratch, Ford had its first 'post-crisis' engine on sale in mid-1975 – the Escort Popular – but the first 'economy' Cortinas were delayed until February 1976. Because the Mk III body style only had months to live, this meant that relatively few were ever built.

The 'economy' Cortina 1300 arrived with a self-satisfied flourish, but was actually a marketing failure. Ford had been so certain it was exactly what the marketplace

The 'works' rally team spent time in 1980 dabbling with a three-litre 'Essex'-engined version of the Cortina Mk V – really a more muscular version of the car being produced in South Africa. Note that it was a two-door car, and the different style of rally wheels, front to rear!

needed that the 'economy' engine was made standard, the previous engine no longer being available.

By any standards, though, this was not a desirable car. The Kent-engined 57bhp 1300 Mk III had been pedestrian enough, but with the new 49.5bhp engine it was a positive traffic block: although a 12 per cent economy gain was possible, this was at the expense of a top speed down to 82mph, and the 0-60mph 'sprint' took 21.5 seconds.

Looking at the engine modifications, one wonders why it all took so long to develop.

Compared with the earlier type, the 'economy' 1300 engine was given an unmodified 1100-type cylinder head, complete with smaller valves and ports, and the latest type of Ford 'sonic-idle' downdraught carburettor.

It was all very well publishing power curves showing that tiny amounts of torque were lost below 4000rpm; the fact was that this made the final Mk III 1300 feel as if it was tied to a tree, and sales fell rapidly away.

As *Autocar* commented when comparing the new with the old:

'The lack of top-end performance was certainly noticeable in higher-speed driving. Putting one's foot down to overtake a lorry from 50mph, the relative lack of urge was very evident, and it took several seconds longer to complete the manoeuvre ... On the steeper Cotswold hills, it felt as though the new car needed a downchange to third before the old one.'

Living on borrowed time

In any case, it was becoming apparent by this time that the Mk III was well into its final year. A

South African specials

Ford's South African factory in Port Elizabeth was set up in the 1920s, and expanded continuously until the 1980s. During that time, tens of thousands of CKD kits were sent out from Ford-UK at Dagenham (body shell sections, running gear, but little trim) although the cars' local content gradually increased over the years. Starting in 1963, a variety of Cortinas were assembled and sold in that country.

Towards the end of the Cortina period, however, a special XR6 version of the Mk IV was developed and marketed, this car being locally designed, only ever built in South Africa, and never officially sold overseas. In the beginning, a limited production 'homologation special,' in effect, was produced, so that Ford-South Africa could have a competitive model for national saloon-car racing, though it then delighted the company by selling better than it could ever have hoped.

This was the engine bay of the 'works' rally development Cortina Mk V, complete with a modified version of the 'Essex' V6 three-litre engine. This project was abandoned at an early stage.

Rather like the British 'Savage' private venture, but unconnected with it, the XR6 used a standard (Capri/Granada) type of 3.0-litre V6 'Essex' engine, with a nominal power output of 136bhp, backed by a Capri/Granada-style gearbox. For motor racing only, there was an optional 200bhp-plus power unit, which had a triple downdraught Weber carburettor installation.

At the end of the 1970s there was a short period when Ford-UK dabbled with developing this car for use in British motorsport (though not as a full-blooded 'works' rally car). One car was tested at Boreham and occasionally rallied, but nothing came of the scheme.

In a country of wide-open spaces, the XR6 was surprisingly popular, and several thousand cars were sold before the entire Cortina range was dropped in 1983, replaced by the Sierra. There were XR6 and XR8 versions of the new-generation models (the latter using a 5.0-litre V8 Ford-USA engine).

Go-faster conversions – Mk III and Mk IV

When the all-new Cortina Mk III came along, John Young, of Super Speed in Essex, wasn't going to mess about with an engine conversion – he developed an engine swop instead! His scheme, like that of Jeff Uren of Race Proved before him, involved dropping the brawny 'Essex' three-litre V6 into the engine bay and beefing up the suspension, then selling it (in 1971) for £312 – raising the total price of a GT-based four-door to £1580.

It wasn't as complete a conversion as you might think, for the 128bhp V6 engine was mated to the existing Cortina 2000 gearbox (which, frankly, was only marginally suitable for that purpose) and to the standard 3.44:1 rear axle. Super Speed also offered an optional 3.22:1 ratio (from the Capri three-litre, costing an extra £25) and an optional ZF limited-slip differential for £50).

There was more: lower front and rear suspension (stiffer at the front), Koni adjustable dampers, different-offset wheels (which gave an extra two inches of track) and competition-type front brake pads.

Performance was almost the same as that of the Savage, with a top speed of 109mph (at 5560rpm, well over the peak for this Capri-style engine), 0-60mph in 9.1 seconds, and about 19 or 20mpg fuel economy. Like the Savage, this car was heavier at the front, which increased the strong understeer already present in this new chassis structure, but it was also a refined and seemingly rugged package.

By the time the same basic conversion was offered in the Mk IV, the engines had been uprated to 138bhp, and the top speed had risen to no less than 117mph. By this time, however, the conversions business was contracting and very few were actually sold.

Another conversion was produced by Willment, where racer Mike Crabtree achieved similar results at similar prices. I am deliberately vague about this because the price of the conversion depended on the axle ratio chosen, while extra engine power was also available in stages, for up to 190bhp.

Super Speed's alternative, for a mere £88 (plus £25 labour to fit) was to offer a two-litre Pinto engine tune-up for the Mk III 2000GT/GXL models. Interestingly enough, John Young claims to have developed the conversion very early in the life of the car, but delayed its introduction by at least a year 'because the interest just wasn't there.'

This was a simple conversion: modified head, 10.0:1 compression, modified inlet manifold, new tubular exhaust manifold and a re-jetted twin-choke Weber. Peak power was not quoted but (using the latest 3.70:1 axle ratio) this car had a top speed of 110mph, 0-60mph in a rousing 8.6 seconds, and could reach 100mph from rest in 31.7 seconds.

new-style Taunus, with a much more angular shape than before (less American-looking, and without the 'Coke-bottle' rear body shape) appeared in January 1976, and Ford made no secret of the fact that there would soon be a very similar 'new Cortina.'

For the Mk III, the end came in midsummer for, as was traditional at Dagenham, the planners took advantage of the July-August holiday 'shutdown' to complete the installation of all the new body press tools and jigs for the next-generation car.

Although it had taken six years rather than four, the Mk III was the third successive Cortina to sell more than a million – all in all, no fewer than 1,126,559 of all types had been built. Would the next Cortina match up to that?

6

CORTINA IV
CO-ORDINATION
WITH GERMANY

Six years after the launch of the 'coke-bottle' Mk III, Ford-of-Europe took the process a stage further. In 1970 a new Cortina and a new Taunus TC had shared a common platform, suspensions, steering, brakes and 'chassis' fittings, much of the running gear and some of the structure; now it was time for near-complete rationalisation.

For the 1977 model year, not only would there be a new – fourth-generation – Cortina, there would also be a new German Taunus, the same in almost every respect. For these new cars, Ford decided to carry over the same basic platform of the Cortina Mk III/Taunus, but to use a new superstructure and style. Not only that, but for the first time the bodies of the new cars – Cortina and Taunus – would actually be the same. In other words, it had taken ten years and two Cortina families for Ford-of-Europe to achieve complete rationalisation in this important mid-size range.

Who bought Cortinas?
When planning the new car, Ford carried out a big market survey, discovering, among other details, that 92 per cent of Cortina customers were married, yet only five per cent of them were women. Three out of four owners had children living at home (which explains why Ford thought interior packaging was important – owners needed the space) and 80 per cent

of them used their cars for holiday transport. Cortina owners, they found, tended to complete about 12,500 miles a year.

They were much more likely to choose such a car for its durability, reliability and quality rather than high performance. Ford also found that owners were looking more and more for longevity, so any new model would have to take that into account. Maybe it wasn't possible to push Cortina sales back up to the 250,000 cars per year mark – there had been more variety in the market place since the 1960s, when such figures had been a normal achievement – but Ford was certainly looking to beat 200,000 cars per year in the mid-1970s.

Most importantly, Ford confirmed what its sales force already knew: that the business sector – crudely, the 'fleet market' – bought or influenced the purchase of more Cortinas than did private customers. Because of the carefully graduated way in which business users tended to reward those provided with cars, this meant that any new Cortina would have to be offered in a myriad of varieties.

There no longer seemed to be much demand for sporting Cortinas, so no provision was to be made for these in the future. As far as Ford and its dealers were concerned, drivers looking for sporty Fords were happy to buy small, nimble Escorts – or racy 2+2 Capris.

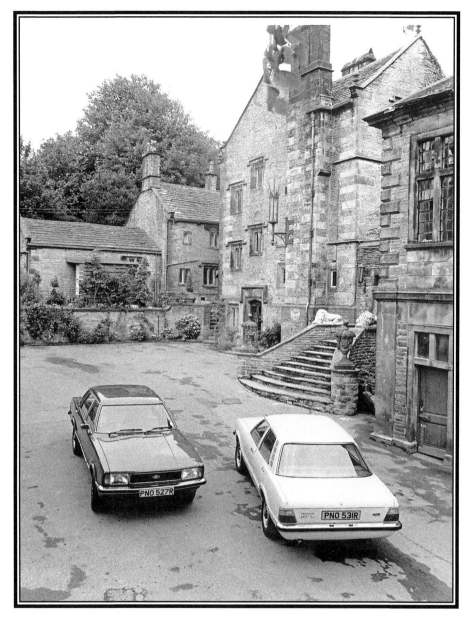

Two views of the new Cortina Mark IV shape developed by Uwe Bahnsen's stylists at Ford-Cologne. The new-generation Ford-Germany Taunus looked identical.

thought that the German Taunus needed more help and more rejuvenation than the British Cortina. At first, therefore, there was no rush to change the British car completely, and there was a serious proposal to keep most of the Mark III's 'coke-bottle' structure and style intact for a 'new Cortina.'

'It was all our own fault,' Sam Toy says. 'Our American colleagues had arrived at the conclusion that: "Well, give it to Britain, because they can sell anything!"'

Although Uwe Bahnsen had recently become the company's head of design (which meant that he controlled the shape of future European Fords), there was still a lot of American influence at Ford-of-Europe. As Harry Calton recalls:

'I remember going to a design proposal meeting where we were looking at proposals for what was to be the Mark IV Cortina. At the time the Taunus was not selling, but the Mark III Cortina was selling very fast, so there was a money-saving half-way-house proposal, which gave the Taunus a completely new style. The Cortina, though, was to have a Mark IV type of front end, but with the Mark III back end preserved.

'We looked at it and said ... well, no thanks!'

The result was that Sam Toy, Terry Beckett and their colleagues demanded, and soon got, approval for the Taunus style to be adopted for the new Cortina. However, because

New style

Design work on a series of new-generation cars actually began in 1973, before the 'facelift' Mark III cars had gone on the market – and even before the Yom Kippur War crisis and its aftermath gripped the world's motor industry by the throat.

Once that had happened, the impact of Yom Kippur, the energy crisis which followed (and its incalculable effect on the world's car-buying habits) meant that Ford immediately had to think hard about the investment it was willing to sink into a new car.

There were other implications. By 1976 (when the new-generation Cortinas were due to go on sale) Ford would just have ploughed hundreds of millions into the launch of the new front-wheel-drive Fiesta, and in 1973-74 no-one could know if demand for the larger Fords would still be high.

In the beginning, there was still a Ford body of opinion which

From three-quarter rear, the Mark IV had a much simpler and somehow more compact style than ever seen on the Mark III, with greatly increased glass area and squared rear profile.

Although the Cortina Mark IV looked significantly smaller than the Mark III which it replaced, this must have been a trick of the styling, as the cars rode on the same platform and wheelbase.

the new Taunus programme was well on the way, and sets of duplicate press tools would be needed for Dagenham's body shop, there would be an inevitable delay. Although the new Taunus would appear early in 1976, the Mk IV Cortina could not possibly go on sale until the autumn of 1976.

In the meantime, Uwe Bahnsen's styling staff had finished a complete platform-up restyle, the result being the crisp and rather angular Mark IV shape. Styling specialists can see certain 'cues' carried forward from the original Fiesta, and it was always obvious that the two cars had come from the same studio in Germany.

Compared with the Mark III, the Mark IV had 15 per cent more glass area (sorely needed) and a much larger rear window – these improvements being all the more marked at the rear – while Ford claimed no less than 310 degrees of all-round visibility. Roof pillars were slimmed down, and there was less exterior ornamentation. For the first time on a Cortina, there was a spoiler under the front bumper.

It was, in many ways, a much more European car than the Mk III, which had always looked like – and was influenced by – what Ford-USA was designing at the time. Although Ford-USA styles were

also sharpening by 1976, Ford-of-Europe was still ahead, and was being allowed to develop its own personality.

If the Mk III, in a way, had always looked larger than it was, the new Mk IV – on the same wheelbase and platform – seemed smaller. Yet both cars were the same length, with a similar-sized cabin. (Aren't stylists clever?)

Most important, though, was the change in the car's attitude, and the improved visibility for driving. In a process first carried out on existing Granadas, the front seats were raised and the front suspension lowered; for the Cortina Mark IV, the nose profile was lowered by nearly three inches, bringing the visibility cut-off point for the road ahead a full four feet nearer the driver. This mattered little at cruising speeds, but seemed to open up new vistas in tight traffic and in parking manoeuvres.

Although there was no obvious external reason why this should be so, the car's high-speed aerodynamic lift was also reduced by ten per cent at front and rear.

The Mark IV's style, in fact, was originally developed only for a new Taunus, and was ready for 'sign-off' before a completely new Cortina Mark IV was approved. This explains, incidentally, why

the new-generation Taunus was unveiled in January 1976, with the Cortina Mk IV delayed by a further eight months.

New-generation Taunus – jumping the gun

Well before Ford-UK was ready to launch a new Mark IV, Ford-of-Germany introduced the new-shape Taunus. If the value-for-money programme for the Cortina Mark III had not been so well received, the new Taunus might have rendered the Mark III a last-season 'lame duck,' but this did not happen.

Ford never actually denied or confirmed that the '1976$^{1}/_{2}$' Taunus was a Cortina clone, but the specialist motoring press soon ferreted out the close relationship. From January 1976, therefore, when the new Taunus appeared at the Brussels Motor Show, the still-secret Cortina Mark IV's cover was blown.

In Brussels Ford PR spokesmen insisted that the next Cortina, when it came, would be an individual with its own character (they would say that, wouldn't they?). Even so, as Stuart Bladon of *Autocar* wrote from Brussels:

'The question of cost, and the

Cortina IV and 1977 model Taunus: a comparison		
Engine	Cortina IV	Taunus (1977 model)
1294cc 'Pinto'	55bhp	59bhp
1298cc 'Kent'	49.5bhp	
1593cc 'Pinto'	59bhp	
		68bhp
	72bhp	72bhp
		88bhp
1993cc 'Pinto'		87bhp
	98bhp	98bhp
1999cc V6 'Cologne'	90bhp	
2293cc V6 'Cologne'	108bhp	108bhp

widely known fact that Britain's Cortina is at the same time overdue for replacement, answers the question for itself ... what we see at Brussels today will be at London in October.'

Mechanically, in fact, there were still major differences between British and German Fords of this size, for each company leaned heavily towards its own preferred choice of engines. As with the Mark III/Taunus TC models, there were engines in the Taunus range which were never to be seen in the UK, as the chart above makes clear.

The principal differences were that no Cortina was ever sold with the 1.3-litre 'Pinto' or the 2.0-litre V6 engine, while no Taunus was ever sold with the 1.3-litre 'Kent' engine.

Although the Taunus range appears to be over-complicated, with too many slightly different engines and power ratings, at this time these cars were supplied to many more markets around Europe than were the Cortinas of the day, some of them requiring particular engine tunes to meet burgeoning exhaust emission regulations.

New style, same chassis

Superficially the Mk IV's chassis and running gear was the same as that of the old Mk III, but it all depends, of course, on what you mean by 'the same.' The layout was, indeed, the same, but almost every area had been revisited and further developed.

The engine line-up was basically the same as for the last of the Mk IIIs, which is to say that it started with a super-economy 49.5bhp 1.3-litre 'Kent' unit and topped out with a 98bhp 2.0-litre 'Pinto', though an 'Economy 1600' with a 59bhp Pinto engine was new. This was Ford's considered response to the energy crisis and its aftermath, as was the smaller engine, yet it was not popular with the clientèle, most of whom were more interested in performance and acceleration.

Except for providing one degree of static negative camber to the wheels – intended to give more tyre 'bite' and reduce understeer – there were no significant changes to the front suspension (to remind you, this featured a coil spring/wishbone layout, very similar to that of current-generation Granadas) but a lot of detail change had been made at the rear.

To complete modifications to the drive line, where the nose of the engine had been lowered further towards the cross-member and therefore the propeller shaft alignment had changed, attachment of the trailing arms to the rear axle had been lowered by 15mm/0.6in, and the trailing arm bushes had been enlarged to provide greater cushioning.

Not only this, but the rear anti-roll bar was 33 per cent stiffer than before, variable-rate rear coil springs were specified and gas-filled dampers adopted for the Ghia and Cortina S versions of the car.

When it was launched, Ford claimed that the fascia designed for the Mk IV had actually been 'pulled ahead' and introduced in 1973 (see Chapter 5, on the facelift process on the Mk III), so there were no changes for the Mk IV itself.

Features such as a sliding sunroof, remote-control driver's door mirror, alloy road wheels, inertia-reel rear safety belts and extremely powerful headlamp washers all became optional for the first time. No longer could a company director view the car and describe it as 'bloody bare,' for the Cortina was moving gradually, but definitely, upmarket in its fourth version.

Ford's worldwide interests were emphasised by the news that the latest cars would not only be built from kits in Australia and South Africa, as before, but also in Ireland (Cork), Portugal and the Far East.

As expected, this was a complicated range, even on announcement (though not all types were available with all engines, and not all were phased into production in the first few weeks). There was the usual mass of two-door and four-door saloons, a five-door estate car, four different engine tunes, and

Base, L, GL, Ghia and S equipment packs.

Although there was no sign of a GT, or especially an E derivative, the S-pack (four-door saloon only) was a novelty which Ford hoped would take over from each of these models. Available only with the 98bhp two-litre engine, the S-pack was really the GL plus a whole lot more – not least 185/70 section tyres, a rev counter, extra driving lamps and 'sports suspension.' The suspension itself not only had gas-filled dampers all round, but stiffer road springs were also fitted at front and rear which were not available on any other version.

A selection of Mk IV prices for the cars which went on sale in October 1976 is shown in the table above.

The transition from Cortina Mk III to Cortina Mk IV was carried out so smoothly at Dagenham that there were virtually no interruptions to the flow of cars out of the gates.

Right from the start the new car took its accustomed place at the head of the British sales charts, and Ford was soon proud to announce that it had taken over as Britain's single best-selling marque.

By this time the assembly plant at Dagenham was bursting at the seams. Although Granadas had been cleared out – henceforth they were all assembled in Germany – the new front-drive Fiesta was being added to the line-up. Day and night shifts were now commonplace,

Mark IV 'S' types not only had boot-lid badges for identification, but also black paintwork across the tail panel and black bumpers with over-riders. Note the 'S' transfer on the front wings.

The swooping coke-bottle shape of the Cortina Mark III's flanks had been eliminated for the Mark IV: the style was simple, more angular, even a touch austere. The front end was simple and effective and was standard on all types, except for touches like over-riders on some models.

Entry-level Mark IV Cortinas were available with two-door bodywork, and were sold without wheel covers, but always with front discs, radial-ply tyres, heated rear window and many other what were once luxury features as standard.

In terms of numbers sold, the GL version was always the most popular of the Mark IV Cortinas. It was the ideal fleet car, selling in hundreds of thousands for the use of middle managers.

The Ghia trim pack was available on Mark IV estate cars fitted with 2.0-litre Pinto or 2.3-litre Cologne V6 engines, the specification including the vinyl roof, tinted glass, and (on 2.3-litre models) special cast alloy road wheels.

with old-fashioned cars and a more damaging history of strikes.

Terry Beckett and Sam Toy were both proud of this success, and the way the market share leapt to 30 per cent and looked like staying there for years to come. Ford-UK had become the dominant partner in Ford-of-Europe – something which Toy always made sure to mention to Chairman Bob Lutz, for Ford-Germany's share was often down below 15 per cent.

'When I was on 30 per cent of the market,' Toy laughs, 'I wasn't under pressure from anybody – USA, management in Europe, or our dealers. That's why there wasn't a single American in the Ford-of-Britain organisation at the time – we didn't need any!'

At last – a V6-engined Cortina

Ford-UK finally introduced a V6-engined Cortina – the 2300GL, 2300S and 2300 Ghia types – in September 1977, more than ten years after the same engine had first been used in a Ford-Germany equivalent, and thirteen years after the first V6 had been put on sale. This was a bold move upmarket, for the 2300 was not only faster and heavier than any other Cortina, but more expensive, too.

Because the Mark IV and the

and some sections of the plant – particularly the press shop – were in continuous (three-shift) operation; more space was needed.

Only three years after the worst of the energy crisis – when the death

of the private car had been widely predicted – the Cortina was selling as never before, and Ford's UK market share kept on rising. This was the period in which Ford pulled well clear of British Leyland, which struggled

The Mark IV estate car was introduced at the same time as the saloons as an integral part of a seventeen-model range. As practical as ever, the estate car could swallow 64 cu.ft of load.

latest Ford Taunus were so similar, development of the British-badged car had been simple, for this was really only a case of building a right-hand-drive V6-engined Taunus, and of making sure that the right-hand steering column could thread its way down alongside the 60-degree V6 engine in the way that the left-hand steering had always done. [This, in any case, was not the largest V6 which would eventually go into this Cortina engine bay – the massive 3.0-litre 'Essex' V6, an entirely different engine, would eventually be used on a locally assembled Ford-South Africa Cortina, the XR6 – see the panel on page 113.]

The original 'Cologne' V6 had been introduced as early as 1964, when a 90bhp/1998cc version had been made available in the new 1965-model Taunus saloons, which had no relation to the original Cortinas. In the years which followed, this engine – eventually enlarged to 2792cc – found a home in several other Ford-Germany models, including the German-built Capri, the German-built Granadas, and all subsequent Taunus ranges.

By the early 1970s this power unit – in racing guise – was also famous for powering the Capri

What a difference fourteen years had made. In 1962 the Cortina was born and Terry Beckett was Ford's Product Planning Manager. In 1976 the fourth-generation Cortina appeared and 'Sir Terence' was now the company's Chairman. Amazingly, in all that time, the Cortina had grown up but had not grown larger.

The 'Cologne' V6 engine was first seen in 1964 as a two-litre unit in a Taunus of an earlier generation, but its first use in a Cortina came in 1977 with the launch of the 108bhp 2.3-litre models. The centrally mounted camshaft was driven from the front of the crankshaft by helical gears: 2.3-litre and 2.8-litre versions were built into British Fords. This is a 2.8 version.

The V6-engined Mark IV was launched in the autumn of 1977, a full year after the Mark IV style had been introduced. Because Ford-Europe had been building V6-engined Taunus models throughout the 1970s (which had the same platform, underpan and engine bay packaging as this Cortina), the rather wide engine fitted easily into the Mark IV engine bay.

RS2600s which won so many European Touring Car races, but whenever Ford-UK spokesmen were asked whether the engine had a future in Britain, the suggestion was usually airily dismissed. Then came Ford-of-Europe rationalisation that implied an end to the use of the heavier British 'Essex' V6 engine, and the decision to use the 'Cologne' V6 in new British-market Fords.

The decision made, the process was unstoppable, and 'Cologne' V6s eventually appeared in British-market Cortinas, Capris, Sierras, Granadas and Scorpios, some as large as 2.9-litres. Cosworth was eventually contracted to produce a superb 24-valve four-overhead-camshaft conversion for use in the 1990s model Scorpios.

I had better make it clear at this stage that, except for sharing the same 60-degree vee configuration, the 'Cologne' V6 engine had nothing in common with the British 'Essex' unit. In the 1960s there had been no attempt to rationalise British and German engineering, and the two engines were designed and developed simultaneously, but were completely different. Compared with the British V6, the 'Cologne' unit was smaller, more compact and lighter and drove its centrally mounted camshaft by gears from the nose of the crankshaft; every casting was different and, as far as I know, there were absolutely no common parts.

Ford-UK could easily have chosen to use the 1998cc *and* the 2293cc 'Cologne' V6s, for these engines were the same size. However, a perfectly satisfactory two-litre 'Pinto' four-cylinder unit was already in use (and was, in any case, more powerful than the two-litre V6), so the company chose to use only the larger size. In standard 108bhp Taunus form, this pushed the Mark IV's top speed to 106mph. At the same time, a 3.44:1 rear-axle ratio was standardised with this engine.

The decision to introduce a Mark IV 2300 was influenced by early sales experience, for in the first year one in three Cortinas was sold with the two-litre/98bhp 'Pinto' engine, and there was constant demand for more of the same. In addition, fleet managers in the late-1970s were tending to allocate their senior managers well-specified smaller cars rather than the traditional large models – and the idea of a V6-engined Cortina Ghia range of saloons and estates was an attractive option.

Because the V6 engine was only 64lb/29kg heavier than the two-litre 'Pinto' unit, only minor changes were needed to the chassis, for S-type front springs, gas-filled dampers and low-profile 185/70-13in tyres did the trick, along with power-assisted steering as standard. Automatic transmission was optional, and was well matched to the lusty low-speed torque of the V6 engine.

Although the 2300 models were more expensive than the 2000s, there was a healthy demand when UK market deliveries began. A comparison of October 1977 retail prices is shown in the accompanying table.

For 1978, therefore, the Cortina range embraced nineteen models, prices ranging from £2523 for the 'base' two-door 1300 to £4795 for the 2300 Ghia Estate. There were four engines, five trim/equipment packs and three body styles. As usual, the problem was not finding a choice of Cortinas in a showroom, but finding exactly the package required.

Maturity

However, the Mk IV was destined to have only a three-year life, for it gave way to the rather different Mk V (or 'Cortina 80') in the autumn of 1979. Although trade booklets like *Glass's Guide* blithely state that there were no changes in that time, such statements contradict Ford's usual policy of tinkering continuously with specifications.

To take advantage of the torque of the 2.3-litre V6 engine, Ford equipped the car with the highest available axle ratio – 3.44:1. Complete with stiffened-up suspension and cast alloy wheels, the 2300S was a very fast car.

V6-engined Cortinas, introduced in 1977, were badged as 2.3 types and sold as 2300S or 2300 Ghia types, with appropriate trim and equipment levels. Both were 100mph cars and were especially smooth in the optional automatic transmission form.

In any case, 1978 was the year in which Ford-UK's Chairman and Managing Director, Terry Beckett, became Sir Terence, and Sam Toy came even closer to the top management position. It was also the year in which the company had to suffer another long pay strike – inspired as much by left-wing political anarchy as by genuine pay grievances – and was forced to close for nine weeks.

One result of the strike was that the 'works' Escort rally cars for the RAC Rally had to be prepared by dealers, private owners and even mechanics in their garages at home; another was that the company's stand at the new NEC (Birmingham) Motor Show was totally empty on opening day, when twenty-eight cars, including the latest Cortina, should have been on display. (This void was eventually filled by Ford's historic vehicles!)

All of which meant that a significant change – the dropping of the 'Economy 1300' engine – passed without comment. From the start of the 1979 model year (from August 1978) the Mk IV's 49.5bhp version of the 1298cc 'Kent' engine was abandoned in favour of the 57bhp version, which had already featured in Mk IIIs from 1970 to the beginning of 1976.

Under the skin the Cortina Mark IV used the same basic platform, suspensions and running gear as the Mark III, but had a new and more angular body shell. Two-door and four-door saloons, plus an estate car, were all available.

In fact, Ford was once again reacting to market forces. There was no point, it concluded, in standardising a 'super-economy' engine at the base of the range if it made the cars uncompetitively slow – and virtually unsaleable.

It was the same old story. After the energy crisis of 1973-74, the media, politicians and the opinionated had all declared what 'the marketplace' needed ... Ford had given it to them in 1976, only to find that 'the marketplace' did not agree.

The 'Economy 1300,' after all, was not only a very slow Cortina, but was probably the slowest UK-market Cortina ever put on sale. The original Cortina 1200 of 1962 had 48.5bhp and weighed only 1725lb, whereas the 'Economy 1300' had 49.5bhp and weighed no less than 2205lb. One bhp more and an extra five hundred pounds of weight – was that progress?

The Mark IV Cortina used the same basic fascia/instrument panel as that first seen on the later model Mark IIIs of 1973-76. The four-spoke steering wheel was initially standard only on GL, S and Ghia versions. Here is a GL, with no rev counter but with a large clock in the main display.

Compare this Mark IV GL interior of 1976 with the interior of a 1962-63 Cortina, and you will see how standards and expectations had rocketed in only fourteen years. By this stage, the GL had reclining front seats as standard equipment.

Top of the range for the new Mark IV Cortina was the Ghia-badged model. (Note the tiny badges on the front wings, just ahead of the doors.) Ghias – only available with 1.6-litre or 2.0-litre engines – were equipped with every possible fitting as standard, including the vinyl roof covering and tinted glass.

Ghia – what's in a name?

There's really no relation between Ghia before Ford took control and Ghia afterwards. Until the 1970s, Ghia was a famous Italian coachbuilder, producing many fine body styles and bodies, in small numbers – including the Maserati Ghibli and a variety of sexy De Tomaso models. Afterwards, it was no more and no less than Ford's Italian (in other words, pan-European) styling house – and a useful name to have around.

The connection, complex and commercially rather turgid, was De Tomaso. The Argentinian-born Alejandro De Tomaso was once a small-time racer who dabbled in making cars. Marrying well – and using his wife's money – during the 1960s, he first of all bought up Ghia, which was in financial trouble. Soon afterwards he snapped up Vignale (another Italian styling house) and then persuaded Ford-USA to back production and selling of the De Tomaso Pantera.

The Ghia badge and trim pack was used for the first time on the Cortina Mark IV, replacing the 'E' pack in the Mark III cars. Not only was there a full-width wood fascia, with matching wood cappings, but a rev counter was standard, along with a centre console which included the analogue clock. This car had the optional automatic three-speed Ford C3 transmission.

By 1973 that relationship had gone sour, the result being that Ford-USA bought the Ghia company and its styling expertise from De Tomaso. Within weeks Ford's own Italian Design Studio had been merged with Ghia, and Filippo Sapino became the Chief Designer.

Ford could then draw on a larger pool of design expertise and decided to use the 'Ghia' name commercially. Starting in 1974 with the Granada Ghia saloons and coupés, and following with the Capri 3000 Ghias and the Escort Mk 2 Ghia, Ford used the famous badge on the top-of-the-line trim and equipment pack of every model line it was making. This invariably replaced an existing trim-pack – in the case of the Cortina, it was the 'E' pack. Please note, however, that 'Ghia' was purely a name – neither the cars nor any of their components were ever actually manufactured inside the old factory in Turin!

For the Mark IV, the GT badging was abandoned, and the 'S' type took over. Like the Mark III GT, the Mark IV had the 98bhp/2.0-litre engine, stiffened-up suspension with gas-filled dampers, rev counter, sports wheels, extra halogen driving lamps and a package of style 'extras', including black bumpers.

Because it was so underpowered for modern traffic conditions, steady speed fuel economy figures came to mean nothing to owners. By pushing hard to keep up with the flow, they used much more of the available acceleration than bigger-engined Cortinas needed, and distorted fuel consumption figures.

Perhaps it's significant that Ford never lent a 1.3-litre engined Cortina Mk IV to the specialist press for road test as its shortcomings would surely have been exposed – and cruelly.

For 1979, therefore, Ford's British array of Cortinas spanned no fewer than twenty-two different models, of which eight were estate types. There was still a two-door saloon in the range (but only with the 57bhp 1.3-litre engine). There were engines from 1.3 litres to 2.3 litres, and prices from £2750 to £5226. Automatic transmission was available on all cars except the 2000S/2300S types, and that was only for marketing, not engineering, reasons.

By any standards, the Cortina Mk IV was a great success, and, along with the Taunus (which did much to rescue Ford-of-Germany from the doldrums), it underpinned the future of Ford's European operation. In the UK, the Cortina was *always* at the head of the charts, often selling twice as fast as any other car except for the Ford Escort. Although the pay strike at the end of 1978 hit the company very hard, by 1979 it was back on top.

Ford, however, was not about to take a rest. After only three years it was ready to make wholesale changes – the Mark V was on the way.

7

CORTINA V
THE FINAL
EVOLUTION

At the end of 1979, a Ford dealer friend of mine summed up the Cortina V perfectly:

'It might look just the same to you, but every skin panel seems to have changed. At least, they all have different Finis Codes (part numbers)!'

Only three years after putting the Cortina Mk IV on sale, in fact, Ford had spent a lot of money – £50 million – on freshening up the range of the last few years. In an earlier Ford era, this would have counted as a mid-life facelift (the Mk I had received one in 1966, the Mk II in 1968 and the Mk III in 1973). This time, however, Ford actually launched the latest car as the 'Cortina 80.' In some aspects – mainly style and body tooling – preparation work had actually begun *before* the Mk IV was unveiled in 1976.

Although Ford tried hard to make the 'Cortina 80' name popular, it was really a waste of time, for within months the public made sure it became unofficially known as the 'Cortina Mk V,' though there was never any badging on the cars to confirm this title. The name that stuck was Mk V, and that is the name I have chosen to give this chapter.

To anyone who complained that the Cortina hadn't changed very much, Ford spokesmen could (and usually did) point out that the formula seemed to be right. In the first six months of 1979, no fewer than 120,000 Mk IVs had been sold, which was as healthy a figure as was ever achieved by earlier cars. In spite of the market gloom cast by the onset of the second energy crisis, there was still a waiting list for all models.

Chairman Sam Toy was asked, during a television interview at the time of launch, whether being a Cornishman had affected the way he ran the company:

'Yes it probably has,' he quipped, 'the average Cornishman has a chip on his shoulder about the size of a block. If somebody from "up country," as we call it, says you can't do something, the Cornishman's immediate reaction, without thinking, is: "Why not?"'

That was why Ford and the Cortina continued to succeed, he thought, and even today he notes that Ford-UK's British market share was then above the 30 per cent mark, a rate not achieved before or since.

If you parked a Mk V alongside a Mark IV, you would notice few changes to the basic proportions, or to the seating package, but detail changes were obvious from all angles: the front grille, rear lamps, roof line and glass outlines were all different ... but this was evolutionary rather than radical. Technically, there were very few important changes introduced for the Mk V, for this was a case of retouching, rather than completely updating, the running gear. It was a

Recognisably the same as the Mk IV, the Mk V (or 'Cortina 80') had a different 'greenhouse' and a modified front end.

process at which Ford was extremely adept.

Body style and structure

The basic platform, structure and layout were those of the Mk IV, but almost every aspect of the detail had been revisited. One of the objectives, it seemed, had been to get rid of weight wherever possible; in fact, Ford claimed that the latest cars were about 40lb/18kg lighter than before.

The new cars didn't look radically different from the Mk IVs (which were dropped after three years and about 600,000 cars) but almost every external panel was different in detail. Certainly, as my dealer friend reminded me, there seemed to be scores of new Finis Codes, and in almost every case a new-type panel would certainly not fit an old-style Cortina.

Part for part, Ford claimed that only the door skin panels were the same as before, though in the case of major pressings, such as wings, bonnet and boot lid, the differences were mainly concerned with mating them up to new grilles, new headlamps and new (much larger) tail lamp clusters.

As seemed to occur so often on Fords of the period, not all the rear-end changes were made to estate car versions, which kept the same unique tail lamps as before ... but I am old enough in the head and so experienced in such Ford matters to know that it was not nearly as simple and straightforward as all that! (Check the parts lists for yourselves.)

The most noticeable change was to the 'glasshouse,' or cabin, where there was an extra six per cent of glass area. Compared to the Mk IV, the upper edges of the door windows had been raised by about 1in/25mm, the windscreen (now laminated on all models for all markets) was made that much deeper to suit, as was the rear (backlight) glass. That inch was enough to mean a brand-new roof pressing, rather flatter in profile than before, along with taller, somehow slimmer rear quarter pillars, which were made to look that way by black air extractor vents along their rear edges.

The rear glass itself also had a different shape at the upper corners: whereas the upper corners of the Mark IV had been rounded, those of the new Mk V had sharp corners. It all helped emphasise the larger glass area of the latest models.

At the front, amber turn indicators were now wrapped around the leading edges of the wings instead of being at the extremities of the front grille, and between the rectangular headlamps there was now a new type of 'aerofoil' front grille, as first seen on the front-wheel-drive Fiesta.

At the rear, stop/tail/indicator lamp clusters were much larger than before, spreading further towards the centre of the car, and including high-density 'fog-guard' lamps for the first time.

All of this and the use of long plastic end caps to both front and rear bumpers, and more prominent body side mouldings on GL and Ghia versions, meant that changes had been made to front and rear wings.

Under the skin and out of sight were new production processes intended to deter rust: four new stages in the paint and finishing programme, wax-injected into closed box sections after painting, and stone-resistant PVC applied to wheelarches and lower body panels. There was also a heavy-duty wax coating sprayed over the entire underbody. These features were not very 'sexy,' or newsworthy, but made the cars likely to be the most durable Cortinas ever put on sale.

Cortina Mk Vs had a different grille, and the side indicators were neatly let into the front corners of the modified front wings. There was more glass area, too.

Inside the car, the package was not changed, though there was a new design of seat. This was not meant to look better, or to be more sporting, but to eliminate the annoying squeak for which the Mk IVs had become famous – or, rather, notorious. [With typical flair, Ford stated that prototype seats had been tested in police cars, involving officers weighing up to 250lb/113kg, with no squeak in evidence after 40,000 miles!]

To improve driver visibility and take advantage of the larger glasshouse, the seats were mounted two inches higher than before. By this time, too, laminated windscreens and inertia-reel front seat belts were standard on all Ford cars.

The fascia/instrument panel display was modified to accommodate face-level fresh-air vents in the centre. This caused a reshuffle of the centre layout, and the introduction (on some models) of a new 'hanging' centre console containing the radio installation.

S-Pack and 'Heavy Duty' pack
The platform, suspension and steering layouts were all carried over from the Mk IV. Further testing, customer reaction, and a continuous accumulation of experience led Ford to re-tune the package. At the same time, the major service interval was extended – from 6000 miles (Mk IV) to 12,000 miles (Mk V).

Compared with the Mk IV, the front springs were softened by nine per cent, while the variable-rate rear coil springs were made five per cent stiffer in initial movement, nine per cent at full load and, to balance all this, the front roll stiffness was restored by fitting a stiffer anti-roll bar. Gas-filled dampers became standard on all models.

At the same time, the Cortina S model, more sporty and with stiffer suspension, disappeared from the range to be replaced by an optional 'S-Pack,' which was available on all but the basic model. (It was also available on estate cars for the first time, though very few such cars were ever built.)

The S-Pack included firmer front and rear coil springs and gas-filled dampers all round, with those at the rear being of larger capacity than the standard items. Alloy road wheels with steel-braced radial-ply tyres were standard, while bumper over-riders, a pair of long-range driving lamps, a rev counter, a four-spoke steering wheel and a specially styled 'hockey-stick' gear knob were all included. On the 2000 models, where it was very popular, the British retail price of this pack was a mere £153; it was cheaper than this on Ghia models because they already had some of the S-pack items as standard.

An alternative 'Heavy Duty Pack' was optional on the 1.3-litre or 1.6-litre Base or L estate cars. Developed from Cortinas

already engineered for some export territories – notably Australia and South Africa – this pack provided 175-13in reinforced radial-ply tyres, uprated suspension settings, a reinforced rear-axle casing and larger rear brake drums. For those who needed this pack, the real bonus was that the authorised maximum payload rose from 935lb/424kg to 1216lb/551kg.

Engine changes
Most of the innovation went into the engine line-up. Although the same basic range – of 1.3-litre 'Kent,' 1.6-litre and 2.0-litre 'Pinto,' and 2.3-litre 'Cologne' V6 – was retained, all had been upgraded, not only to make them more powerful but more fuel-efficient than before.

In 1975, don't forget, Ford had laid down a strategy which was to make its models 15 per cent more fuel-efficient by the end of the decade, and this was the final push towards that objective. (Since then, of course, increasingly strict exhaust emission regulations have also made their mark.)

In each and every engine, the old-type positively driven plastic fans were discarded and replaced by multi-bladed plastic fans mounted on viscous couplings with thermostat drive controls. When the engines were cold, the fans merely milled lightly round, but as the engine warmed up and fed heat into the fan hubs, tension increased and positive drive was

This was the Ghia version of the Cortina Mk V, complete with the latest style of cast alloy road wheels.

Basic 1980 Mk V model combinations				
Engine/body	Equipment Pack			
	Base	L-Spec	GL-Spec	Ghia-Spec
1300 2-door	x	x		
1300 4-door	x	x		
1600 4-door	x	x	x	
1600 Estate	x	x	x	
1600 (Weber) 4-door				x
1600 (Weber) Estate				x
2000 4-door			x	x
2000 Estate			x	x
2300 4-door			x	x
2300 Estate			x	x

taken up. Whatever the engine temperature, by this method fan speeds were limited to no more than 3000rpm – worth up to 2bhp at peak revs.

Each engine type was modified in different ways:

1.3-litre 'Kent'
The old-type Ford/Motorcraft carburettor of the Mk IV was replaced by a single-choke Ford/Motorcraft instrument, of new design called a Variable Venturi (or VV) which Ford claimed succinctly to be its response to the rival SU and Zenith-Stromberg constant vacuum types.

The result was an increase in peak power from 57bhp (Mk IV) to 61bhp (Mk V). The super-economy version with 49.5bhp was no longer on offer.

1.6-litre 'Pinto'
The same new type of Ford VV carburettor was fitted to the basic 1.6-litre 'Pinto,' with a claimed 30 per cent reduction in carbon monoxide (CO) exhaust emissions, and a boost of peak power from 72bhp (Mk IV) to 75bhp (Mk V).

In addition there was to be a new high-output version of this engine, which would be fitted only to the 1600 Ghia saloons and estates. It came with a more sporty overhead camshaft profile, and a downdraught compound dual-choke Weber carburettor. This was

rated at 92.5bhp, slightly lower than the near-identical Weber-carburetted 'Pinto' (95bhp) fitted to the Mk 2 Escort RS Mexico of 1976-78, but better than the 88bhp unit fitted to Cortina Mk IIIs.

2.0-litre Pinto
Apart from the package of friction-reducing internals used on all Pinto models, which included a reduction in valve spring loading, the improvements – from 98bhp (Mk IV) to 102bhp (Mk V) – were due entirely to the addition of the viscous fan.

2.3-litre 'Cologne' V6
At this time there were more changes to the German-manufactured V6 than to any of the other Cortina power units, which goes a long way to explaining the power boost from 108bhp (Mk IV) to 116bhp (Mk V).

Not only had the viscous fan been standardised, but there were cylinder head improvements, larger valves, a higher compression (9.0:1 instead of 8.75:1), changes to the camshaft timing, recalibrated carburettor and ignition settings, and breakerless transistorised ignition.

Engines, transmissions and equipment packs
By this period the Cortina model range was always a triumph of product planning and computer-aided manufacture. As before, there

were to be two-door or four-door saloons and an estate car, five different petrol engines, manual or automatic transmissions, and a choice of four equipment packs.

The basic model combinations for the 1989 Mk V are shown in the table above.

To add yet further complications, Ford C3 automatic transmission was available on all except 1300 'Base' models!

These were the details of the Cortina 80/Mk V equipment packs:

Base: Specification included reclining front seats, engine temperature gauge, inertia-reel front seat belts, heated rear window, reversing lamps, mat in boot compartment, door mirror (driver's side only), pressed-steel wheels with 165-13in radial-ply tyres, black bumpers.

L-Spec added: Cloth seat trim, carpets instead of rubber mats, cigarette lighter, upper part of centre console, lockable glovebox, halogen-bulb headlamps, brightwork bumpers, body-side tape strips.

GL-Spec added: Seat head restraints, map pockets on the door trim panels, clock, trip distance recorder, four-spoke steering wheel, full centre console, coin rack – useful for parking meters, tolls, etc) – front-seat passenger's vanity mirror, rear-seat centre arm rest, sports road wheels, woodgrain instrument surround, body-side moulding instead of a tape strip.

Ghia-Spec added: Head rest pad inserts, cut-pile carpet, cloth sidewalls in door trims, wood cappings on door window sills, map pockets in front seat backs, rev counter, light in fascia glovebox, remote-control lever for driving door mirror, lamp in boot, cast-alloy road wheels, 185/70-section tyres, bumper over-riders.

Mk V on the market

This was a complicated range, even on announcement, for there were no fewer than twenty derivatives in the UK list in September 1979, of which eight were estate cars. The table shows how the saloons lined up (four-door unless indicated).

Ford realised that an exaggerated advertising campaign was not needed. (This would, in any case, have impressed no-one after all these years.) The company concentrated first, therefore, on engineering and service improvements. There wasn't

1300	Base 2-door	£3346
	Base	£3475
	L 2-door	£3677
	L	£3806
1600	Base	£3675
	L	£4006
	GL	£4394
	Ghia	£5237
2000	GL	£4634
	Ghia	£5380
2300	GL	£5243
	Ghia	£5989

The last – and most popular – special-edition Cortina was the Crusader of 1982, with the optional two-tone colour scheme. Available engine sizes were 1300, 1600 and 2000.

an ounce of hype in the specialist magazine adverts but a lot of detail concerning reliability, durability and reduced service costs.

This must be one of the most boring headlines ever conceived:

'The new Ford Cortina – engineered to be reliable, economical, responsive ...'

By 1981 the Cortina was still one of Britain's best-selling cars, and worldwide CKD production reached a new high with 750 cars a day being assembled from kits supplied by Dagenham. Nonetheless, industry watchers must have realised that the car was moving towards retirement when the first Cortina Mk V 'Special Edition' – the Carousel-

was launched in June 1981.

Looking back from a period in which almost every manufacturer – even Rolls-Royce – produces 'special edition' or 'limited edition' versions of its cars, it's amazing it took Ford so long to embrace the 'special-edition' Cortina philosophy. There had been a rare 'Olympic' Mk III in 1976, but in nineteen years of production that was all.

Then, in the last year there were two: the Carousel and the Crusader (which followed in 1982).

Carousel, Crusader, and changes for 1982

Like all such limited editions, the Cortina Carousel was a dressed-up version of a more humble model – in this case the 1.3-litre or 1.6-litre Standard. Mechanically there were no changes, but trim and equipment were boosted with Ford claiming eighteen extra features.

Only 6000 Carousels – saloons and estate cars – were built, with every one having a two-tone colour scheme (three combinations), sports road wheels, door mirrors on both doors, Cortina L seats, door trims and head restraints, and many Cortina GL features, including the fascia and centre console.

Then (this was Ford, don't forget!) there were options, which included tinted glass, an electrically operated radio aerial, and (for estate cars only) a tailgate wash/wipe.

Carousel prices were: 1.3 saloon £4540, 1.6 saloon £4780, 1.6 estate £5250.

For 1982 (but announced in September 1981) the Cortina range was given a final equipment reshuffle. Adjustable head restraints were standardised (except on Base models), the L received a modified fascia, while the Ghia version was given engine compartment and boot lamps. Other upgrades included Recaro front seats as options on the S-pack, L and GL models.

The Crusader derivative of April 1982 – as we now know a car launched in the last few months of the Cortina's life – came to be named in a very strange way. Although it was only the second-ever Cortina 'special-edition' car, please note that

the Crusader was not a 'limited-edition' product, for no fewer than 30,000 were built in the spring and summer of 1982.

In the late 1970s Ford had gained very valuable fleet-car business from Trafalgar House Investments, a company which then controlled the *Daily Express* newspaper. Although the *Express* habitually backed British-owned companies, there had been a falling out between Chairman Victor Matthews and British Leyland, which was never resolved.

Matthews and Sam Toy became great friends, and as the Cortina approached its end in 1982, a fruitful offer was made:

'The Taunus had already died in Germany, and the Cortina was starting to struggle,' Toy told me. 'David Benson of the *Express* talked to his editor, he talked to Victor Matthews, and the result was this amazing offer – if it would help us, we could use the *Express* "Crusader" emblem, and there wouldn't be any trademarking problems.'

Once again, it seems, Ford and the Cortina had been lucky, for this gave a final boost to the car's image, and no extraordinary discounting action was needed later in 1982.

In many ways the Crusader was really a 'Carousel Mk 2,' for it was also founded on the Base model and had many of the same additional equipment, though this time there was also to be a 2000 version. Special features of the

Cortina 1300L	£5060
Crusader 1300	£5160
Crusader 1600	£5435
Cortina 1600GL	£6054
Crusader 2000	£5755
Cortina 2000GL	£6384

Crusader were bonnet pin-striping, body-side tape decals, wheel rim embellishers, Ghia-styled seats in Durham velour trim, cut-pile carpets and a long centre console which incorporated a radio. This time the two-tone paintwork was an optional extra.

It was quite obvious that Ford intended the Cortina to go out with a bang, for the Crusader's prices told their own story. The table shows how the single-tone Crusader four-door saloons compared with the normal versions.

P100 – the Cortina pick-up

Surprisingly enough, as far as the British market was concerned, one entirely new Cortina model remained to be announced – in July 1982, only weeks before the private-car range would disappear. This was the P100 pick-up truck, a version of which had already been in production at Ford-South Africa in Port Elizabeth for several years, was set to continue for some time, and was now to be marketed in the UK for the first time. Significantly, UK market P100s had a 10in/254mm longer wheelbase than the first

South African types to allow a much larger loading area.

Manufacturing arrangements were complex. For the 1.6-litre 'Pinto' engine, some electrical components and some body panels – about 35 per cent of the total value, by cost – were shipped out to South Africa, while the rest of the P100 was made there.

The P100 only had a bench seat. As far as the rear of the doors, the style was like that of the Cortina Mk V saloon, but much of the front underframe was strengthened, and everything rear of the cab was special – the 15-gallon/68-litre petrol tank was positioned behind the cab, and instead of a coil spring rear suspension, there was an old-fashioned (but rugged) half-elliptic spring back end instead.

In every way this was a more muscular machine than the private car, for the maximum possible payload was 2431lb/1103kg, the maximum allowable weight being a whopping 5240lb/2377kg. The Pinto engine was in its standard Mk V tune with 75bhp, and was matched to the same basic gearbox, though fitted with wider ratios (as found in Granada Diesel models).

As everyone who has employed a variety of local builders and tradesmen will know, the P100 went on to be a very successful vehicle for small businesses, and remained on the market for many years in the 1980s.

1980 Taunus – like for like changes ...

In parallel with the Cortina Mk V, there was a modified Ford-of-Germany Taunus, as there had been for the Cortina Mk IV. As before, the cars looked the same, and in most cases actually *were* the same; once again, however, the Germans stayed loyal to their own engine line-up. Like the Cortina Mk V, the latest Taunus had uprated engines across the board, and the range continued to use the 1.3-litre 'Pinto' and the 2.0-litre V6 'Cologne' engines, which never found their way into British Cortinas.

As in previous years, however, the final version of the Taunus never sold as well as the Cortina, and by 1982 it was almost dead in the water. Fortunately for Ford, the Genk factory could be kept busy building Transit vans for a time, but this is not a period which Ford-of-Europe remembers with pride.

When the Cortina finally retired in the summer of 1982, so, too, did Taunus production at Genk. During the 1980s, Ford-of-Germany had much less freedom: its next model would be the same as the Ford-UK version – and would be called 'Sierra.'

The Cortina bows out

Months before the end, Ford had admitted publicly that the Cortina Mk V was to be replaced – not by a new-generation Cortina but by a totally different type of car which would carry the model name of Sierra.

A show car, titled Probe III, made this very clear for, as *Autocar* commented in its Probe III analysis of September 1981:

'It will be interesting to see eventually how much of the thinking revealed this week is put into practice for the Cortina after the new model is introduced next year ...'

The answer was already known, unofficially, to many of the press (no sneak previews, scoops or embargo breaking in those days!). Much of Probe III, which was based on the Sierra style, would feature in the 'next Cortina.' Except that it would not be called Cortina, after all.

There seemed to be no lack of demand, nonetheless, for the 1982 model year Cortinas, and for the Crusader 'run-out' models in particular, for sales and production carried on at full spate at Dagenham until midsummer.

By this time, in any case, the well-loved Cortina was a British motoring icon for which no-one had a bad word. To anticipate its passing, the BBC TV arts programme *Arena* devoted an entire programme to the Cortina in January 1982, calling it a classic masterpiece in steel and plastic.

It was not, of course, a serious study of the car, but a tongue-in-cheek, rather irreverent view of the model. Ford and Cortina owners seemed to take the programme in good part. The entire film was

The writing was on the wall for the Cortina when Ford showed this Probe III car in 1981. Under the modified style there was a new-generation Sierra platform and running gear. The bi-plane spoiler was intended for the XR4i.

linked by comedian Alexei Sayle and it included a poem by the Poet Laureate, Sir John Betjeman. The opening lines of *Executive*, in fact, encapsulate so well some of the reasons behind the Cortina's success:

"I am a young executive. No cuffs than mine are cleaner;

I have a slim-line briefcase and I use the firm's Cortina.

In every roadside hostelry from here to Burgess Hill

The maîtres d'hôtel all know me well and let me sign the bill."

By the summer of 1982, however, the Cortina's British career was almost at an end. Although it was not publicised

until the very week that the Sierra was launched, the last British-built Cortina had been assembled at Dagenham on Thursday 22 July, suitably heralded, suitably placarded, and driven off the track by Ford's Chairman Sam Toy.

For the next few weeks which included the traditional 'shut-down' holiday period Dagenham was in turmoil as Cortina facilities were torn out and replaced by those for the Sierra – but in the showrooms, customers were only barely aware of this.

Tens of thousands of Cortinas were still available, and although sales perked up to take account of the new 'Y-reg.' number plates, any number of special deals, incentives and sweet part-exchange

arrangements were available to shift the balance. As far as I can see, all were sold before the end of 1982.

Because of the pipeline effect, and the time it took for the last CKD packs to be shipped abroad and assembled in local factories, the Cortina was still available in Australia and South Africa until 1983, but after that it really was all over.

Now it was time for the figures to be added up and new targets set for future models. When all the statistics had been totalled, no fewer than 4,279,079 Cortinas of all types had been manufactured – making this family a best-seller by any standards.

Sierra – the Cortina's replacement

Soon after the Cortina dropped out of production, the new Sierra hatchback took its place. Then, as later, its jelly-mould style and general character caused controversy. Over the years, the Sierra would also sell in millions – but it never achieved the success of the Cortina.

Ford's product planners wanted to develop a new car to replace the Cortina and the Taunus, with an assembly of cars to be concentrated at Dagenham and Genk in Belgium. Although Ford-UK lobbied long and hard for the 'Cortina' name to be retained, it was seen as a British – rather than a pan-European – name.

In addition, the legacy of the Taunus (still seen as a stodgy failure in Germany) had to be resolved, so a new name was decided upon: 'Sierra' took over from both types. Although the new product was extensively researched by Product Planning, the Sierra was always seen as the pet project of Bob Lutz of Ford-of-Europe.

Lutz, ex-BMW, wanted to push the middle-sized Ford further upmarket, and although he takes credit for the advanced, all-independent-suspension chassis, he must also take the blame for the controversial style and image:

'The day we launched the Sierra,' Sam Toy says, 'one of our largest fleet-car customers, Imperial Tobacco, said to me: "Don't we get a notchback?" and when we said no, they immediately told us we had lost their fleet order.'

That was just one of several shocks caused by the arrival of the Sierra (which had no notchback version until 1987). In any case, Sierra build quality was below standard in the first year or so and there was a notorious problem with high-speed stability in side-winds, all of which hit Ford hard. Tens of thousands of fleet sales, in particular, went to the Vauxhall Cavalier, a disaster from which Ford never recovered.

This was the original Sierra, the car which took over from the Cortina in 1982. At one time, Ford had considered keeping the Cortina name, but was probably wise not to. Except for the engine and transmission range, almost everything in the Sierra was new. An era had come to an end.

8

TODAY'S CORTINAS
KEEPING THEM
ON THE ROAD

There is good news and bad news. The good news is that the stock of nicely preserved Cortinas now seems to be going up, not down, while the bad news is that owners need a lot of patience and perseverance just to keep them like that. For every beautifully restored Cortina, another thousand have gone to the great Ford scrapyard in the sky.

Amazingly, though, a number of newly restored, good-condition cars still seem to be coming on to the market. In the UK, waiving the road tax on cars more than twenty-five years old has encouraged owners to put such cars back into service. In some cases enthusiasts have spent years rebuilding, or even recreating, an old Cortina, and are ready to sell it on for a remarkably reasonable price. They would like to make more money, of course, but market forces – your reluctance to pay more – won't let them.

Although there were many more Cortinas on the road in the 1980s than there are today, the survivors tend to be in better overall condition – and often look more original. Cortinas, like all such mass-produced machines, gradually went downmarket as they got older. Then they went through the usual period of neglect, through the era of weird colours, fluffy dice and fake leopard-skin seat covers, but most have now returned to their original roots.

The miracle is that so many cars have managed to survive at all. Although Ford built well over four million Cortinas between 1962 and 1982, there is very little after-sales support from the factory today. To those who think that this is scandalous, I would merely point out that the original Cortina was conceived nearly fifty years ago, and that the very last were sold fifteen years before this book was written. In fairness, it's perhaps a bit unreasonable to expect a forward-looking factory to take much interest after all this time.

Ford applies a sliding scale to parts supply for cars which have dropped out of production. As a general rule, it guarantees to stock spare mechanical parts for out-of-production cars for ten years after the last one has been built, but it will only guarantee to stock carpet, trim and other related cloths and furnishing for the first three years.

All such laws, however, are there to be broken, or stretched. Don't assume, for example, that a call to your dealer just a week before the ten years is up will find parts ready and waiting for your order – that part may already be no longer available (or NLA, the dreaded term known to all club parts specialists!). On the other hand, there have been instances where continuing – and therefore profitable – demand has been such that some items are still to be found many years after their 'sell-by date' has passed.

135

Cortinas thrive today through one-make clubs – the Mk I Owners' Club caters for all versions of the original car.

In any case, if you approach the sort of dealer whose parts specialists really know their stuff, are benevolent and interested in keeping the 'classic' machinery on the road, he may be able to suggest the use of more modern parts which are interchangeable and have superseded those originally developed for Cortinas. (They won't tell the purists if you don't!) Some dealers, however, are better than others ...

Ford, however, recognises the strength of the 'classic' movement, and that its older models attract so much attention these days. To make sure that all relevant queries are handled by the same people, Ford asks one of its employees, John Nevill of the Public Affairs department, to act as the conduit between the clubs, club members, and every Ford department.

John's job title – Heritage Fleet Administrator – tells its own story, for he looks after the Ford collection of historic vehicles. You can contact him on the telephone at: 01277 253308. John provides invaluable liaison services for clubs, especially with Ford's own patents office, which has to approve reprinting any literature or re-manufacture of any parts to official patterns, tools or drawings. His organisation also provides regalia and other PR/ publicity support for club events, and brings individuals, cars and clubs together:

Previous contact Derek Sansom

told me: 'You would be amazed how many Cortina owners call me and don't even know that particular clubs exist. In any case, I reckon that 90 per cent of such callers are reluctant even to join a club – maybe it's because they don't want to be regimented, or maybe they think the expense isn't going to be worth it.

'What they don't realise is that club membership fees can usually be saved, many times over, by savings on finding parts, or on things like insurance costs ...'

Before starting to write this chapter, and to get a feel for the situation, I made a point of talking to enthusiasts in the Cortina Mk I Owners' Club – on the basis that the oldest Cortinas would be the most difficult to maintain and restore. This club confirmed that Ford's Parts Division could no longer supply any important components for 'their cars,' and that there is really no point in approaching a Ford dealer either.

One of today's problems is that the majority of British Ford main dealers have redeveloped their business in the last two decades – not only in the showroom area, but also in the workshops and

parts stores. In many cases this has meant a complete upheaval in the way they stock and administer parts. Although it is occasionally possible to find a traditional dealer who has still kept a few old-car parts in a dusty corner of his stores, the phrase 'rocking horse droppings' springs to mind.

Ford, like every other manufacturer of mass-production cars, guarantees expertise and parts supply for a period after any model has been dropped; for Cortinas this period has long gone. Although many dealers still employ mechanics and parts technicians who were familiar with the cars of that period, today's dealers will probably not even have an old parts microfiche, or repair manual, in the back of a cupboard.

This is where the one-make clubs come in. In almost every case, they have a number of truly expert owners – those invaluable characters who can recite colour and trim combinations, know what engines were also shared with other Ford cars, and what pieces of suppliers' kits are still to be found.

Not only that, but the one-make clubs have usually found rare copies

The one-make clubs have made sure that Cortinas can usually be restored. This rusty old body shell ...

... eventually looked as good as new, though thousands of hours of private-owner dedication were needed to ensure that.

of parts lists, owners' manuals and workshop manuals, which they use as bibles. In some cases (the Mk I Owners' Club is one) they have obtained official permission from Ford to reprint them, and these can prove invaluable.

Although permission to reprint is usually granted, Derek Sansom told me, Ford expects club officers to contact him to ask before they do it.

Having decided not to stock parts any more, Ford, has been extremely helpful over re-manufacture. Sometimes, in the case of parts which were supplied to them, rather than made 'in-house' (badges, brightwork, electrics and chassis components are cases in point), they have often been able to bring clubs and suppliers together. On occasion they have even allowed their own tooling (rare) or drawings (much more frequently) to be used.

To get a feel for this, I talked to Malcolm Rugman, Spares Secretary of the Cortina Mk I Owners' Club. His task – unpaid and hard work – was to run the spares system in the club, which includes locating old stock, finding new supplies of parts and looking after re-manufacture.

In many cases he has not been able to arrange re-supply, and has had to arrange for replica parts to be made. Ten years ago, at the end of the 1980s, Cortinas were being scrapped because essential replacement items were not available:

'We always try to keep a good supply of what we call "MoT" items in stock, which means that our members can always keep their cars on the road – bushes, dampers, exhaust systems, and the appropriate structural panels.'

This club, and others not quite as large, was then ambitious enough to go into body panel re-manufacture. By 1997 most major panels – not Ford-sourced, but made on new and very accurate press tooling – had become available for two-door, four-door and estate car types:

'We have also had bonnet, door and boot lid panels pressed in aluminium, not only for ourselves, but also for any Lotus-Cortina owner who needs them!'

This business has grown so much that panel sales – whether of complete or repair panels – accounts for at least two-thirds of all parts sales. Everything, really, except for major roof pressings and some minor panels, is now available once

again, and the Club takes it as a challenge not to be beaten.

Re-manufacture of other items – rubber buffers, mountings and trim items, for example, is going ahead all the time. Every investment has to be justified from club funds, so there are limits to what is possible. Compared to 1982, when the club was founded, progress has been enormous.

'Getting glass seems straightforward enough,' Malcolm told me. 'There is a company, Autosparks, which produces wiring looms, we have started remaking trim items, we tend to get chrome items re-chromed because we can't get spares, but some items are very difficult.'

Malcolm's experience is typical, according to those Cortina club members I have consulted: getting body and trim parts is now much more difficult than getting hold of mechanical and other chassis components. Parts supply problems, in general, can therefore be split into two areas – body items (where supply of original factory-produced items is next to impossible) and mechanical items (where significant numbers of drive-train, suspension, steering and braking components are still available).

Each breed of Cortina has its own specific corrosion problems. In all cases, though, the chassis legs and bulkhead joints give trouble, as do the joints between inner and outer wings. This is a 1990s-restored shell, now back on the road with a proud owner.

The floor pan on this Cortina shell was in such awful condition that it had to be cut away and renewed. One side is repaired, the passenger-side floor being next.

In one form or another, engines, gearboxes and axles for Cortinas were shared with so many other Ford models, in so many different ways, that there has been enough demand for Ford to keep many of them available for a long time.

Although many pre-cross-flow engine parts (1962-67) have virtually disappeared, cross-flow (or 'Kent') supplies are much easier to get hold of, for these engines were built in many millions, and were also used in all types of rear-wheel-drive Escorts, in Capris and even in some versions of the first-generation, front-drive Fiestas.

The single-overhead-camshaft Pinto engines of the 1970s and 1980s were also used in some rear-wheel-drive Escorts, Capris and Granadas, and also in the 1980s generation of Sierras (which replaced the Cortina). Since the last of these engines was not built until the end of the 1980s, component supply in the 1990s is still good.

In the UK the German-built 2.3-litre V6 engines (as found in Mark IV and Mark V Cortinas) were only shared with Granadas of the period (though they were found in large numbers in German-built Capris and Taunus models) and so supplies are limited.

Similarly, the all-synchromesh manual gearboxes originally developed for the Cortinas were also found in Capris and a few Escorts (though most Escorts had a light-duty transmission not usually found in Cortinas), along with four-cylinder-engined Granadas of the period.

However, there were differences in internal ratios from model to model, so don't rush into the 'scrapyard' solution when building a Cortina without making investigations first. In the UK, at least, steering-column-change versions of this gearbox were always rare, and parts for the external linkage are now scarce indeed.

The Anglia 105E of 1959-67 had an earlier type of gearbox, without synchromesh on first gear, which was never found in any Cortina. Today's Cortina enthusiasts tend to shy away from automatic transmissions, which is probably just as well. Rebuilds from specialists are possible (of the original Borg Warner Type 35, or of the later Ford C3 variety) but these come at very high cost, and new supplies have completely dried up.

Cortina rear axles were originally of the 'English' (or 'Timken') type, as used in many Anglias and Escorts, though from the 1970s the higher-powered versions were sometimes found with a German-sourced axle

known within Ford as the 'Salisbury' axle (which was entirely different in construction and detail).

Complete axles are no longer available; however, as these were also used on Anglias, Escorts and Capris, components to rebuild both types are still available. Remember, though, that there was a whole variety of axle ratios, and because tracks varied, so did the length of the axle casings themselves.

It should always be possible to return a Cortina to 'as new' condition, mechanically, especially for club members who know how to use sources to acquire parts. However, the basic problem with these cars, as with all Fords of the period, is that although well-maintained running gear seemed to go on for ever, the body shells tended to rust from an early age. Corrosion on these cars was certainly unsightly, and it could be life-threatening when passing MoT tests was required.

Where does a Cortina body go rusty ? These cars were always built down to a price, engineered in the days when expensive rust protection was not built in to the original production process, so the answer is – everywhere, but most especially around the highly stressed areas which have to withstand suspension loads. On Mk I and Mk II types, this means the strut turret tops and the rear spring hangers, while on Mk III/IV/V types this means chassis

In some cases, a patch or repair panel is enough to restore a wing to health.

If you want to carry out a do-it-yourself Cortina restoration, you must be prepared for careful, panel-by-panel replacement. The floor pan of this car may not be repairable, but first the sills – inner and outer – need replacing. By modern standards, however, the Cortina is a simple design.

In this case a complete inner wheelarch assembly (or 'A' panel) has been grafted into place, along with that vital piece of metal, the turret top mounting. All such panels have been remanufactured by enterprising one-make clubs.

legs (front and rear) and rear suspension mountings.

Each and every club has experts who have experienced every horror story regarding Cortina corrosion, so it is as well to consult them at an early stage – ideally, even before you go out to buy a car of your own. Later cars – Mk IVs and Mk Vs in particular – were better built and better protected than the earlier-generation types, and it is also true that thoroughly restored examples of any type are often in better condition than the original.

Remember, though, that Ford never built the Cortina to be an heirloom. If you can turn *your* Cortina into one, you are to be congratulated!

Clubs and specialist magazines

So-called 'classic car' magazines all over the world now recognise certain Cortina models as cars worth keeping, cherishing and restoring, and there is certainly more coverage of these cars today than ever before. The fact that Lotus and GT-engined examples always figure strongly in old car rallies (some as long and demanding as the Peking-to-Paris Motor Challenge of 1997) means that they gain publicity all for themselves.

One particular magazine, *Classic Ford*, deserves special mention – and I'd better admit that I have a particular interest as a regular contributor. It is published

by Kelsey Publishing, a magazine house with an impressive range of specialist titles. *Classic Ford* developed out of *Ford Heritage*, first as a series of one-off issues in the early 1990s; later as a six-times-a-year magazine. Inaugurated in 1997 as its successor, and also appearing six times a year, *Classic Ford* became so popular that it was published monthly from the spring of 1998. It gives its fair and colourful share of attention to Cortinas and other models in related Ford families.

Read it regularly and you will not only learn about the cars themselves, but will pick up tips on restoration, trouble-shooting, parts supply and – where appropriate – updating and modernisation of the type.

Classic Ford is stocked by all good newsagents, but to be sure of getting a regular supply you might consider taking out a subscription. In which case they can be contacted at the following address:

Classic Ford Customer Service Team,
Kelsey Publishing Ltd,
Cudham Tithe Barn,
Berry's Hill,
Cudham,
TN16 3AG

subs@kelsey.co.uk
Phone: UK – 0333 0439848
International – 0044 1959 543747

Every year, incidentally, *Classic Ford* is linked with a colossal outdoor show – 'Ford Fair' – which is usually held on a Sunday in August, often at a race circuit so that owners can take their cars out on the track too. By any measure, this is one of the very largest one-make events on the British enthusiast/classic car scene. If the weather is good, between 12,000 and 15,000 people attend, and Cortinas are always well represented. Every Cortina owner should try to go along, if only to meet his mates, to call in at the various one-make club displays and to browse among the dozens of trader stands.

Then, of course, there are all the dedicated one-make clubs which each cater for one type of Cortina. As I have already detailed, these have their own ways of re-manufacturing or re-sourcing parts for their particular cars, each of them holds at least one major outdoor event during the summer.

There seems to be such a regular and rapid turnover of club officers in all these organisations that it seems unwise to give full contact addresses, for they will

A fine display of Lotus-Cortinas at a mid-1990s club meeting. Fellowship like this helps to ensure that such cars will always survive.

Ford owners' clubs

Mk1 Cortina Owners' Club
Cortina Mk I Owners' Club of Australia
Lotus-Cortina Register
Ford Cortina Mk2 & 1600E Owner's Club
Ford Cortina Mk 2 Owners' Club
Mark Three Owners' Club
Ford Cortina Owners' Club Mk1-5
Pre 67 Ford Owner's Club
Cortina Owners' Club of Ireland
Classic Cortina Car Club (New Zealand)
Cortina Club Norway
Swedish Ford Cortina Club

Did Cortinas look as good as this when Ford first built them? They may be non-standard – those are Minilite-style alloy wheels, for example – but the authentic spirit survives.

inevitably be out of date even before this book is published!

However, since most of them advertise in *Classic Ford*, and that magazine regularly publishes a list of the latest contacts, you shouldn't be in the dark for long. One sure way to find out, of course, is to ask another Cortina owner, who will surely have joined at least one club already.

In some cases there is more than one club for a particular car, almost certainly because there has been a 'breakaway' movement to start a rival organisation. There were at least a dozen Cortina-orientated clubs at the last count. Opposite is a complete list of UK-based national clubs which welcome Cortina owners.

Please remember, however,

that clubs rise and fall. When you read this, new clubs may have been founded, while some of the smaller ones listed may have died away. My apologies – but classic car motoring is like that.

CORTINA

APPENDIX I
**WHAT HAPPENED
WHEN?**

Spring 1960:	Project work on 'Archbishop' began.
October 1962:	Introduction of original 1.2-litre Cortina Mk I.
January 1963:	Introduction of 1.5-litre Cortina Super. Preview of twin-cam Lotus-Cortina (sales began mid-year).
April 1963:	Introduction of Cortina GT.
October 1964:	Mid-life facelift, including first-ever 'Aeroflow' Cortina fascias.
June 1965:	'Leaf-spring' Lotus-Cortina replaced original 'coil spring' version.
October 1966:	Introduction of Cortina Mk II, direct replacement for Cortina Mk I.
March 1967:	Introduction of Lotus-Cortina Mk II.
October 1967:	New bowl-in-piston 'Kent' engine fitted to all except Cortina-Lotus.
October 1968:	Mid-life facelift all models, and single-rail gearbox update for transmission.
September 1970:	Introduction in Germany of Ford-Germany Taunus, based very closely on the Cortina Mk III platform, but with modified styling, two-door coupé style and different engine line-up, including 1294cc overhead-cam 'Pinto,' 1999cc V6 and 2293cc V6 'Ford-Cologne' engines, none ever used in Ford-UK Cortina Mk IIIs. [This car not sold in UK.]
October 1970:	Introduction of Cortina Mk III, direct replacement for the Cortina Mk II, with entirely new platform/chassis/style, and 'Pinto' overhead-cam engines.
September 1973:	Mid-life facelift, with new fascia style and engine realignment. Overhead-valve 'Kent' engine finally replaced by 1.6-litre 'Pinto' engines. Introduction of 2000E model.

February 1976:	Introduction in Germany of Ford-Germany Taunus, on which next generation Cortina (Mk IV) to be based. New style on Cortina Mk III platform, but different engine line-up, including 1294cc overhead-cam 'Pinto' and 1999cc V6 'Ford-Cologne' units, neither ever fitted to Ford-UK Cortinas. [This car never sold in UK.]
October 1976:	Introduction of Cortina Mk IV, direct replacement for Cortina Mk III, very closely related to the Ford-Germany Taunus of February 1976. Same basic platform as Mk III, but new body style like new Ford-Germany Taunus.
October 1977:	Introduction of 2300 model, with 108bhp/2293cc V6 Ford-Cologne engine.
September 1979:	Introduction of Cortina Mk V (unofficial name – Ford preferred 'Cortina 80') as development of Cortina Mk IV. Same platform and basic structure as Mk IV, many detail panel changes. Same engine line-up but all engines uprated.
September 1982:	End of Cortina assembly in UK. Overseas assembly from CKD kits continued until 1983 while stocks lasted. New Sierra range replaced Cortina Mk V, immediately in UK and from 1983 in other markets.

CORTINA

APPENDIX II
ENGINES

Cortina Engines – UK market cars

So many different petrol engine tunes were used over the years that a chart tells the story best:

UK market cars

Four-cylinder engines
Overhead-valve, pre-cross-flow

1198cc	48.5bhp	1962-66
1298cc	53.5bhp	1966-67
1498cc	59.5bhp	1963-66
1498cc	61bhp	1966-67
1498cc	78bhp	1963-66

Overhead-valve, cross-flow

1298cc	49.5bhp	1976-78
1298cc	57bhp	1970-76
		1978-79
1298cc	58bhp	1967-70
1298cc	61bhp	1979-82
1599cc	68bhp	1970-73
1599cc	71bhp	1967-73
1599cc	88bhp	1967-70

Single overhead camshaft

1593cc	59bhp	1976-79
1593cc	72bhp	1973-79
1593cc	75.5bhp	1979-82
1593cc	88bhp	1970-73
1593cc	92.5bhp	1979-82
1993cc	98bhp	1970-79
1993cc	102bhp	1979-82

Twin overhead camshaft

1558cc	105bhp	1963-66
	109bhp	1967-70

V6-cylinder engines

2293cc	108bhp	1977-79
	116bhp	1979-82

Note: This chart does not include engines with slightly different power outputs, which were listed for special export markets.

CORTINA

APPENDIX III
PERFORMANCE

Cortina performance summary

So many different Cortinas were produced in twenty years that there simply isn't enough space to give every performance figure for every version. Here, then, is a summary for the most significant saloon models:

Model	Engine size/ (bhp)	Max speed (mph)	0-60 mph (secs)	Standing ¼ mile (secs)	Overall fuel consumption (mpg)
Cortina Mk I					
1200	1198/48.5	76.5	22.5	22.4	30.2
1500 Super	1498/59.5	80.8	19.0	20.8	27.2
1500GT	1498/78	94	13.9	18.7	26.2
Lotus	1558/105	106	9.9	17.4	20.8
Cortina Mk II					
1100 Cross-flow	1098/49.5	71	27.1	23.7	22.3
1300	1298/53.5	81	21.4	22.2	26.8
1300 Cross-flow	1298/57.5	84	18.2	20.7	24.9
1600 Cross-flow	1599/64	83	16.7	20.3	26.7
1600E	1599/88	98	13.1	18.8	25.1
Lotus	1558/109	104	11.0	18.2	22.2
Cortina Mk III					
1300	1298/57	85	19.8	21.4	24.8
1600	1599/68	92	14.7	19.7	24.6
1600 (OHC)	1593/72	93	15.1	19.9	23.7
1600GT	1593/86	98	13.3	19.0	25.3
2000	1993/98	105	10.7	18.1	25.1
2000E	1993/98	102	10.6	17.7	24.1
Cortina Mk IV					
1600	1593/72	93	13.7	19.4	27.4
2000	1998/98	100	11.0	17.9	24.1
2300 (Auto)	2293/108	99	12.2	18.8	22.8
Cortina Mk V (Cortina 80)					
1600	1593/75.5	91	13.6	18.9	29.3
2000	1993/101	102	10.3	17.7	29.2
2300 (Auto)**	2293/116	103	10.5	18.0	24 (Est)

Except where noted, these figures were all recorded by *Autocar* magazine when the particular model was current.

** Tested in *Autosport*.

CORTINA

APPENDIX IV
PRICES

Cortina prices – on announcement

All prices are UK retail, complete with purchase tax. Entry-level prices are quoted in each case.

Cortina Mk I

October 1962:	1200 saloon	£573
January 1963:	1500 Super saloon	£670
	Cortina-Lotus	£1100
April 1963:	1500 GT	£749

Cortina Mk II

October 1966:	1300 saloon	£669
	1500 saloon	£706
	1500GT saloon	£810
March 1967:	Cortina-Lotus	£1068
October 1967:	1300 'cross-flow' saloon	£724
	1600 'cross-flow' saloon	£767
	1600GT 'cross-flow' saloon	£865
	1600E saloon	£982

Cortina Mk III

October 1970:	1300 saloon	£914
	1600 (OHV) saloon	£961
	1600GT (OHC) saloon	£1112
	2000 saloon	£1027
October 1973:	2000E saloon	£1638

Cortina Mk IV

October 1976:	1300 saloon	£1950
	1600 (Economy) saloon	£2153
	1600 saloon	£2291
	2000 saloon	£2696
November 1977:	2300S saloon	£3527

Cortina Mk V (Cortina 80)

September 1979:	1300 saloon	£3503
	1600 saloon	£3848
	2000 saloon	£4839
	2300 saloon	£5474

The last series of listed prices for these cars was as follows:

October 1982:	1300 saloon	£4515
	1600 saloon	£4972
	2000 saloon	£6384
	2300 saloon	£7207

The most expensive Cortina listed at this time was the 2300 Ghia Estate, which retailed at £8614 – or at £9070 if the optional automatic transmission was fitted.

APPENDIX V
PRODUCTION

Cortina production figures – 1962-83

Ford-UK and its associates have built millions of cars over the years, but have not preserved all their detail build records. Although I would love to be able to quote chapter and verse on every Cortina sub-derivative, this is simply not possible.

Cortinas were built in four European factories, while KD (knocked down) kits from Dagenham were sent for final assembly to countries such as Australia and South Africa. Here, as preserved by Ford-UK, are the year-on-year assembly statistics:

Year	Dagenham	Genk (Belgium)	Amsterdam	Cork (Ireland)	Lotus	KD	Totals
1962	49,365					17,685	67,050
1963	203,277					61,055	264,332
1964	159,543				3,301**	62,135	224,979
1965	192,383					70,970	263,353
1966	182,200					60,171	242,371
1967	249,861		4,151			36,960	290,972
1968	208,410		25,378			27,600	261,388
1969	201,340		23,976			40,575	265,891
1970	145,865		15,025			34,488	195,378
1971	140,602		13,261			28,318	182,181
1972	221,085		20,792			22,350	264,227
1973	165,541		18,775			35,850	220,166
1974	139,917		16,915			29,450	186,282
1975	110,743		3,267			27,050	141,060
1976	123,608					22,770	146,378
1977	132,075	8,189		6,862		29,580	176,706
1978	111,513	33,989		8,487		32,160	186,149
1979	138,173	72,310		18,206		44,640	273,329
1980	133,506	35,571		17,341		32,905	219,323
1981	91,846	67,192		16,440		32,050	207,528
1982	54,308	49,416		9,508		33,750	146,982
1983						5,500	5,500
Totals	3,155,161	266,667	141,540	76,844	3,301	788,012	4,431,525

**There is an obvious 'compression' here. According to this computer print-out, every one of the Lotus-Cortina Mk I models was built in 1964! This is wrong – as production stretched from 1963 to 1966. However, I have not attempted to modify the figures.

Here are other summaries of the production of each Cortina type:

Mk I (1962-66)
Total production	1,013,391

Which includes:
Standard saloon	34,514
De Luxe saloon	704,871
De Luxe estate	108,219
Super saloon	77,753
Super estate	7,786
1500GT saloon	76,947
Cortina-Lotus	3,301

Mk II (1966-70)
Total production	1,024,869

Which includes:
Standard saloon (2-door)	14,324
Standard saloon (4-door)	4,914
De Luxe saloon (2-door)	251,537
De Luxe saloon (4-door)	347,462
Super saloon (2-door)	18,950
Super saloon (4-door)	116,143
Estate cars	90,290
GT (1500 & 1600) (2-door)	62,592
GT (1500 & 1600) (4-door)	54,538
1600E (2-door)	2,563
1600E (4-door)	57,524
Cortina-Lotus	4,032

Mk III (1970-76)
Total production	1,126,559

Which includes:
Saloon (2-door)	143,420
Saloon (4-door)	824,068
Estate cars	154,216
Pick-up models (not sold in the U.K.)	4,855

Mk IV (1976-79) and Mk V (1979-82)
Total production (combined)	1,131,850

This summary totals 4,296,669 – rather different to the 4,431,525 quoted for the year-on-year figures. Pity the poor historian!

All I can say is that both sets of figures have been provided in good faith by different Ford archives at different times.

CORTINA

APPENDIX VI
SPECIFICATIONS

Cortina Mk I – 1200, 1500 and 1500GT (1962-66)

Layout
Unit-construction body/chassis structure with steel panels. Two-door or four-door four-seater saloon or five-door estate (not GT), front engine/rear drive, choice of trim packs

Engine	1200	1500	1500GT
Block material	Cast iron		
Head material	Cast iron		
Cylinders	4 in-line		
Bore and stroke	80.96 x 58.17mm	80.96 x 72.8mm	80.96 x 72.8mm
Capacity	1198cc	1498cc	1498cc
Main bearings	3	5	5
Valves	2 per cylinder, operated by in-line overhead valves, pushrods and rockers, with camshaft mounted in block, driven by chain from crankshaft (all)		
Compression ratio	8.7:1	8.3:1	9.0:1
Carburettor	Solex B30 PSEI-2	Zenith 33VN	Weber 28/36 DCD.1
Max. power	48.5bhp (net) @ 4800rpm	59.5bhp (net) @ 4600rpm	8bhp (net) @ 5200rpm
Max torque	63lb.ft. @ 2700rpm	81.5lb.ft. @ 2300rpm	97lb.ft. @ 3600rpm

Transmission			
	Four-speed manual gearbox, all-synchromesh (all)		
Clutch	Single dry plate, hydraulically operated (all)		
Overall gearbox ratios			
Top	4.13	3.90	3.90
3rd	5.83	5.51	5.51
2nd	9.88	9.34	9.34
1st	14.62	13.81	13.81
Reverse	16.35	15.46	15.46
Final drive	4.13:1	3.90:1	3.90:1

Note: The 1200 Estate car had a 4.44:1 final drive ratio – all intermediate ratios being similiarly modified. Three-speed automatic transmission was optional with the 59.5bhp/1,498cc engine for 1964:

Overall transmission ratios:	
Direct	3.90 (all)
Intermediate	5.66 (all)
Low	9.32 (all)
Reverse	8.15 (all)
Maximum torque multiplication	2.00 (all)
Final drive	3.90:1 (all)

Suspension and steering

Front	Independent, coil springs, MacPherson struts, anti-roll bar, telescopic dampers (all)		
Rear	Live (beam) axle, by half-elliptic leaf springs, hydraulic telescopic dampers (all)		
Steering	Recirculating ball (all)		
Tyres	5.20-13in cross-ply	5.60-13in	5.60-13in
		(6.00-13in on estate car)	

	1200	1500	1500GT
Wheels			
Rim width	Steel disc, bolt-on (all)		
	4.0in (all)		
Brakes			
Type	Drum brakes at front and rear,	(ditto 1200)	Disc brakes at front,
	Hydraulically operated	(ditto 1200)	drums at rear,
Size	8.0 x 1.75in front drums (9.0in x 1.75in	(ditto 1200)	9.5in front discs,
	on 1500 and estate car), 8.0 x 1.5in	(ditto 1200)	9.0 x 1.75in. rear drums
	rear drums		

Dimensions (in/mm)	
Wheelbase	98/2209mm (all)
Track	
Front	49.5/1257mm (all)
Rear	49.5/1257mm (all)
Overall length	168.3/4275mm (170.5/4331mm with over-riders) (all)
Overall width	62.5/1587mm (all)
Overall height	56.6/1435mm (all)

Unladen weight	From 1725lb/782kg	From 1842lb/835kg	From 1750lb/794kg

Cortina Mk II – 1300, 1500 and 1600

Layout

Unit-construction body/chassis structure, with steel panels. Two-door or four-door four-seater saloon, or five-door estate car

Engine	1300	1300 B-I-P	1500	1600
	Original type	**B-I-P type**	**Original type**	**B-I-P type**
Block material	Cast iron (all)			
Head material	Cast iron (all)			
Cylinders	4 in-line (all)			
Bore and stroke	80.96 x 62.99mm	80.96 x 62.99mm	80.96 x 72.8mm	80.96 x 77.62mm
Capacity	1298cc	1298cc	1498cc	1599cc
Main bearings	5	5	5	5
Valves	2 per cylinder, operated by in-line overhead valves, pushrods and rockers, with camshaft mounted in block, driven by chain from crankshaft (all)			
Compression ratio	9.0:1	9.0:1	8.3:1	9.0:1
Carburettor	Ford GPD	Ford GPD	Ford GPD	Ford GPD
Max. power	53.5bhp (net) @ 5000rpm	58bhp (net) @ 5000rpm	61bhp (net) @ 4700rpm	71bhp (net) @ 5000rpm
Max. torque	71lb.ft. @ 2500rpm	71.5lb.ft. @ 2500rpm	88.5lb.ft. @ 2500rpm	91.5lb.ft. @ 2500rpm

Transmission	Four-speed manual gearbox, all-synchromesh (all)			
Clutch	Diaphragm spring, cable operated (all)			
Overall gearbox ratios				
Top	4.125	4.125	3.89	3.89
3rd	5.80	5.80	5.51	5.51
2nd	9.87	9.87	9.34	9.34
1st	14.55	14.55	13.81	13.81
Reverse	16.28	16.28	15.46	15.46
Final drive	4.125:1	4.125:1	3.89:1	3.89:1
Three-speed automatic transmission				
Direct	4.125	4.125	3.89	3.89
Intermediate	5.96	5.96	5.64	5.64
Low	9.45	9.45	9.30	9.30
Reverse	8.59	8.59	8.15	8.15
Maximum torque				
multiplication	2.00	2.00	2.00	2.00
Final drive	4.125:1	4.125:1	3.89:1	3.89:1
	(Saloon only)			

Suspension and steering	
Front	Independent, coil springs, MacPherson struts, anti-roll bar, telescopic dampers (all)
Rear	Live (beam) axle, by half-elliptic leaf springs, telescopic dampers (lever-arm dampers on estate cars (all)
Steering	Recirculating ball (all)
Tyres	5.20-13in cross-ply to 6.00-13in cross-ply, depending on engine and model (all)
Wheels	Steel disc, bolt-on
Rim width	4.0in (4.5in rim optional) (all)

Brakes	
Type	Disc brakes at front, drum brakes at rear, hydraulically operated (all)
Size	9.00in front discs, 8.0 x 1.5in rear drums (all)

Dimensions (in/mm)

Wheelbase	98.0/2490mm (all)
Track	
Front	52.5/1330mm (all)
Rear	51.0/1300mm (all)
Overall length	168.0/4267mm (all)
Overall width	64.9/1650mm (all)
Overall height	56.5/1440mm (all)
Unladen weight	From 1898lb/861kg (all)

Cortina Mk II – GT (1966 – 1970)

(Cross-flow B-I-P 'Kent' engines were fitted from late 1967)

Layout

Unit-construction body/chassis structure with steel panels. Two-door or four-door four-seater saloon, front engine/rear drive. Estate car to special order from late 1967

Engine	Original	BIP Kent Engine
Block material	Cast iron (all)	
Head material	Cast iron (all)	
Cylinders	4 in-line (all)	
Bore and stroke	80.96 x 72.8mm	80.96 x 77.62mm
Capacity	1498cc	1599cc
Main bearings	5	5
Valves	2 per cylinder, operated by in-line overhead valves, pushrods and rockers, with camshaft mounted in block, driven by chain from crankshaft (all)	
Compression ratio	9.0:1	9.0:1
Carburettor	Weber 28/36 DCD.1 dual-choke	Weber 28/36 DCD.1 dual-choke
Max. power	78bhp (net) @ 5200rpm	88bhp (net) @ 5200rpm
Max. torque	97lb.ft. @ 3600rpm	96lb.ft. @ 3600rpm

Transmission

	Four-speed manual gearbox, all-synchromesh (all)
Clutch	Diaphragm spring, hydraulically operated (all)

Overall gearbox ratios

	Original	From January 1967
Top	3.90	3.90
3rd	5.51	5.45
2nd	9.34	7.84
1st	13.81	11.59
Reverse	15.46	12.95
Final drive	3.90:1	3.90:1

Suspension and steering

Front	Independent, coil springs, MacPherson struts, anti-roll bar, telescopic dampers (all)
Rear	Live (beam) axle, by half-elliptic leaf springs, radius arms, hydraulic telescopic dampers (all) Radius arms deleted from 1968
Steering	Recirculating ball (all)
Tyres	5.60-13in cross-ply (optional 165-13 radial ply at first, standard from late 1967 (all)
Wheels	Steel disc, bolt-on (all)
Rim width	4.0in. (4.5in with radial ply tyres) (all)

Brakes

Type	Disc brakes at front, drum brakes at rear, hydraulically operated (all)
Size	9.62in front discs, 9.0 x 1.75in rear drums (all)

Dimensions (in/mm)

Wheelbase	98/2209mm (all)
Track	
Front	52.5/1334mm (all)
Rear	51.0/1295mm (all)
Overall length	68.0/4267mm (all)
Overall width	64.9/1648mm (all)
Overall height	56.5/1435mm (all)
Unladen weight	From 1955lb/887kg (all)

Cortina-Lotus Mk I and II (1963 – 1970)

Layout
Unit-construction body/chassis structure with steel panels, some light-alloy panels in 1963 – 1965. Two-door four-seater saloon, frontengine/rear drive

Engine

Block material	Cast iron (all)	
Head material	Cast aluminium (all)	
Cylinders	4 in-line (all)	
Bore and stroke	82.55 x 72.8mm (all)	
Capacity	1558cc (all)	
Main bearings	5 (all)	
Valves	2 per cylinder, operated by twin overhead camshafts mounted in cylinder head, and inverted tappets. Camshafts driven by	
chain	from crankshaft (all)	

	Mk I	**Mk II**
Compression ratio	9.5:1	9.5:1
Carburettors	Twin Weber	Twin Weber
	40DCOE dual choke.	40DCOE dual choke.
Max. power	105bhp (net) @ 5500rpm	109bhp (net) @ 6000rpm
Max. torque	108lb.ft. @ 4000rpm	106lb.ft. @ 4500rpm

Transmission

	Four-speed manual gearbox, all-synchromesh (all)	
Clutch	Single dry plate, hydrauulically operated	Diaphragm spring, hydraulically operated

Overall gearbox ratios
(Original)

Top	3.90 (all)	
3rd	4.79 (all)	
2nd	6.39 (all)	
1st	9.75 (all)	
Reverse	10.96 (all)	
Final drive	3.90:1 (all)	

(From July 1964 – October 1965)

Top	3.90 (all)	
3rd	5.51 (all)	
2nd	7.96 (all)	
1st	13.82 (all)	
Reverse	15.46 (all)	
Final drive	3.90:1 (all)	

(From October 1965)

Top	3.90	3.77
3rd	5.45	5.28
2nd	7.84	7.58
1st	11.59	11.20
Reverse	12.95	12.52
Final drive	3.90:1	3.77:1

Suspension and steering

Front	Independent, coil springs, MacPherson struts, anti-roll bar, telescopic dampers (all)	
Rear	(Original): Live (beam) axle, by coil springs, A-bracket, radius arms, hydraulic telescopic dampers	
	(From June 1965): Live (beam) axle, by half-elliptic leaf springs, twin radius arms, hydraulic telescopic dampers	
Steering	Recirculating ball (all)	
Tyres	6.00-13in cross-ply	165-13in radial ply
Wheels	Steel disc, bolt-on.	Steel disc, bolt-on
Rim width	5.5in	5.5in

Brakes

Type	Disc brakes at front, drum brakes at rear, hydraulically operated (all)	
Size	9.5in front discs,	9.62in front discs,
	9.0 x 1.75in rear drums	9.0 x 1.75in rear drums.

Dimensions (in/mm)

Wheelbase	98/2209mm	98/2209
Track		
Front	51.5/1308mm	53.5/1359mm
Rear	50.5/1288mm	52.0/1321mm
Overall length	168.3/4275mm	168.0/4267mm
Overall width	62.5/1587mm	64.9/1648mm
Overall height	53.75/1365mm	55.7/1415mm
Unladen weight	1820lb/825kg	2025lb/963kg

Cortina Mk III (1970 – 1976)

Layout

Unit-construction body/chassis structure with steel panels. Two-door or four-door four-seater saloon, or five-door estate car

	1300 Kent 1600 Kent 'Kent' engined cars		1600 GDP Pinto 'Pinto' engined cars	1600 pinto	2000 Pinto
Engine					
Block material	Cast iron (all)				
Head material	Cast iron (all)				
Cylinders	4 in-line (all)				
Bore and stroke	80.96 x 62.99mm	80.96 x 77.62mm	87.65 x 66mm	87.75 x 66mm	90.8 x 76.95mm
Capacity	1298cc	1599cc	1593cc	1593cc	1993cc
Main bearings	5	5	5	5	5
Valves	2 per cylinder, operated by in-line overhead valves, pushrods and rockers, with camshaft mounted in block, driven by chain from crankshaft		2 per cylinder, operated by opposed overhead valves and rockers, with single overhead camshaft mounted in cylinder head, driven by internally cogged belt from crankshaft		
Compression ratio	9.0:1	9.0:1	9.2:1	9.2:1	9.2:1
Carburettor	Ford GPD	Ford GPD	Ford GPD	Weber 32/36 DGAV	Weber 32/36 DFAVH
Max. power	57bhp (net) @ 5500rpm**	68bhp (net) @ 5200rpm	72bhp (net) @ 5500rpm	88bhp (net) @ 5700rpm	98bhp (net) @ 5500rpm
Max. torque	67lb.ft. @ 3000rpm**	85lb.ft. @ 2600rpm	87lb.ft. @ 3000rpm	92lb.ft. @ 4000rpm	111lb.ft. @ 4000rpm
Transmission	Four-speed manual gearbox, all-synchromesh (all)				
Clutch	Diaphragm spring, cable operated (all)				
Overall gearbox ratios					
Top	4.11	3.89	3.89	3.89	3.444
3rd	5.80	5.48	5.45	5.45	4.72
2nd	9.87	9.34	7.82	7.82	6.78
1st	14.55	13.77	13.93	13.93	12.57
Reverse	16.28	15.40	12.91	12.91	12.59
Final drive	4.11:1	3.89:1	3.89:1	3.89:1	3.444:1
Three-speed automatic transmission, optional on:					
Direct		3.89	3.89	3.89	3.444
Intermediate		5.64	5.64	5.64	4.99
Low		9.30	9.30	9.30	8.23
Reverse		8.15	8.15	8.15	7.21
Maximum torque multiplication		2.00	2.00	2.00	2.00
Final drive		3.89:1	3.89:1	3.89:1	3.444:1

** Note: From February 1976 to the end of production in summer 1976, the 1300 specifications were altered to 'economy' settings. Compared with the above, differences were as follows: 1300: 49.5bhp (net) at 5000rpm. Maximum torque 64lb.ft. at 3000rpm

Suspension and steering

Front	Independent, coil springs, wishbones, anti-roll bar, telescopic dampers (all)
Rear	Live (beam) axle, by coil springs, trailing and semi-trailing radius arms, telescopic dampers (all) Anti-roll bar on some models (all)
Steering	Rack and pinion (all)
Tyres	5.60-13in cross-ply to 185/70-13in radial-ply, depending on engine and specification pack chosen
Wheels	Steel disc, bolt-on (all)
Rim width	4.5in to 5.5in, depending on tyres and wheel pack chosen (all)

Brakes

Type	Disc brakes at front, drum brakes at rear, hydraulically operated (all)
Size	9.62in front discs, 8.0 x 1.5in rear drums ('Kent' engined cars), 9.0 x 1.75in rear drums ('Pinto' engined cars)

Dimensions (in/mm)

Wheelbase	101.5/2581mm (all)
Track	
Front	56/1522mm (all)
Rear	56/1422mm (all)
Overall length	168.0/4267mm (all)
Overall width	67/1703mm (all)
Overall height	52/1321mm (all)
Unladen weight	From 2083lb/945kg (all)

Cortina Mk IV (1976 – 1979)

Layout
Unit-construction body/chassis structure with steel panels. Two-door or four-door four-seater saloon, or five-door estate car

Engine

Engine	'Kent' engine	'Pinto' engined cars			Cologne V6 engine
Block material	Cast iron	Cast iron			Cast iron
Head material	Cast iron	Cast iron			Cast iron
Cylinders	4 in-line	4 in-line			60-degree V6
Bore and stroke	80.96 x 62.99mm	87.65 x 66mm	87.75 x 66mm	90.8 x 76.95mm	90.0 x 60.1mm
Capacity	1298cc	1593cc	1593cc	1993cc	2293cc
Main bearings	5	5	5	5	4
Valves	2 per cylinder, operated by inline overhead valves pushrods and rockers with camshaft mounted in block driven by chain from crankshaft	2 per cylinder, operated by opposed overhead valves and rockers with single overhead camshaft mounted in cylinder head, driven by internally-cogged belt from camshaft			2 per cylinder, operated by in-line overhead valves, pushrods and rockers, with camshaft mounted in Vee of block, driven by gears from crankshaft
Compression ratio	9.2:1	9.2:1	9.2:1	9.2:1	8.75:1
Carburettor	Ford GPD	Ford GPD	Ford GPD	Weber 32/36 DGAV	Solex twin-choke 35/35 EEIT
Max. power	49.5bhp (net) @ 5000rpm **	59bhp (net) @ 4500rpm	72bhp (net) @ 5000rpm	98bhp (net) @ 5200rpm	108bhp (net) @ 5000rpm
Max. torque	64lb.ft. @ 3000rpm **	82lb.ft. @ 2600rpm	87lb.ft. @ 2700rpm	111lb.ft. @ 3500rpm	130lb.ft. @ 3000rpm

***For the 1979 model year (August 1978 onwards) there was also an alternative engine tune: 57bhp (net) @ 5500rpm, 67lb.ft. @ 3000rpm**

Transmission
Transmission	Four-speed manual gearbox, all-synchromesh
Clutch	Diaphragm spring, cable operated

Overall gearbox ratios

Top	4.11	3.78	3.89	3.75	3.444
3rd	5.75	5.29	5.45	5.24	4.72
2nd	8.26	7.60	7.82	7.39	6.78
1st	14.71	13.53	13.93	13.69	12.57
Reverse	13.64	12.55	12.91	13.73	12.59
Final drive	4.11:1	3.78:1	3.89:1	3.75:1	3.444:1

Three-speed automatic transmission

Direct			3.89	3.75	3.444
Intermediate			5.72	5.51	5.06
Low			9.61	9.26	8.51
Reverse			8.21	7.92	7.27
Maximum torque multiplication			2.04	2.04	2.04
Final drive			3.89:1	3.75:1	3.444:1

Suspension and steering
Front	Independent, coil springs, wishbones, anti-roll bar, telescopic dampers (all)
Rear	Live (beam) axle, by coil springs, trailing and semi-trailing radius arms, anti-roll bar, telescopic dampers (all)
Steering	Rack and pinion (power-assisted on V6-engined models, optional power-assistance on 2-litre models from 1977) (all)
Tyres	165-13in to 185/70-13in radial-ply, depending on engine and specification pack chosen (all)
Wheels	Steel disc, bolt-on (all)
Rim width	4.5in to 5.5in, depending on tyres and wheel pack chosen (all)

Brakes
Type	Disc brakes at front, drum brakes at rear, hydraulically operated (all)
Size	9.75in front discs, 8.0 x 1.5in rear drums (1300 and 1600-engined cars), 9.0 x 1.75in rear drums (2000 and 2300-engined cars)

Dimensions (in/mm)
Wheelbase	101.5/2581mm (all)
Track	
Front	56.9/1445mm (all)
Rear	56/1422mm (all)
Overall length	170.3/4326mm (all)
Overall width	67/1703mm (all)
Overall height	52/1321mm (all)
Unladen weight	From 2205lb/1000kg (all)

Cortina Mk V [Cortina '80'] (1979 – 1982)

Layout

Unit-construction body/chassis structure with steel panels. Two-door or four-door four-seater saloon, or five-door estate car

	1300 'Kent' engine	1600 Ford VV 'Pinto' engined cars	1600	2000	2300 V6 Cologne V6 engine
Engine					
Block material	Cast iron	Cast iron			Cast iron
Head material	Cast iron	Cast iron			Cast iron
Cylinders	4 in-line	4 in-line			60-degree V6
Bore and stroke	80.96 x 72.8mm	87.65 x 66mm	87.75 x 66mm	90.8 x 76.95mm	90.0 x 60.1mm
Capacity	1298cc	1593cc	1593cc	1993cc	2293cc
Main bearings	5	5	5	5	4
Valves	2 per cylinder, operated by in-line overhead valves, pushrods and rockers, with camshaft mounted in block, driven by chain from crankshaft	2 per cylinder, operated by opposed overhead valves and rockers, with single overhead camshaft mounted in cylinder head, driven by internally-cogged belt from crankshaft			2 per cylinder, operated by in-line overhead valves, pushrods and rockers, with camshaft mounted in Vee of block, driven by gears from crankshaft
Compression ratio	9.2:1	9.2:1	9.2:1	9.2:1	9.0:1
Carburettor	Ford VV	Ford VV DGAV	Weber 32/36 DGAV	Weber 32/36	Solex twin-choke 35/35 EEIT
Max. power	61bhp (net) @ 6000rpm	75.5bhp (net) @ 5500rpm	92.5bhp (net) @ 5900rpm	102bhp (net) @ 5400rpm	116bhp (net) @ 5500rpm
Max. torque	68lb.ft. @ 3000rpm	87.5lb.ft. @ 2800rpm	93lb.ft. @ 4000rpm	114lb.ft. @ 4000rpm	131.5lb.ft. @ 3000rpm

Transmission	Four-speed manual gearbox, all-synchromesh
Clutch	Diaphragm spring, cable operated

Overall gearbox ratios

Top	4.44	3.78	3.89	3.45	3.444
3rd	6.35	5.29	5.33	4.73	4.72
2nd	9.72	7.60	7.66	6.80	6.78
1st	16.25	13.53	14.20	12.59	12.57
Reverse	18.82	12.55	14.24	12.62	12.59
Final drive	4.44:1	3.78:1	3.89:1	3.45:1	3.444:1

Three-speed automatic transmission

Direct		3.89	3.89	3.45	3.444
Intermediate		5.72	5.72	5.07	5.06
Low		9.61	9.61	8.52	8.51
Reverse		8.21	8.21	7.28	7.27
Maximum torque multiplication		2.04	2.04	2.04	2.04
Final drive		3.89	3.89:1	3.75:1	3.444:1

Suspension and steering

Front	Independent, coil springs, wishbones, anti-roll bar, telescopic dampers (all)
Rear	Live (beam) axle, by coil springs, trailing and semi-trailing radius arms, anti-roll bar, telescopic dampers (all)
Steering	Rack and pinion (power-assisted on V6-engined models, optional power-assistance on 2-litre models) (all)
Tyres	165-13in to 185/70-13in radial-ply, depending on engine and specification pack chosen
Wheels	Steel disc, bolt-on (all)
Rim width	4.5in to 5.5in, depending on tyres and wheel pack chosen.

Brakes

Type	Disc brakes at front, drum brakes at rear, hydraulically operated (all)
Size	9.75in front discs, 8.0 x 1.5in rear drums (1300 and 1600-engined cars), 9.0 x 1.75in rear drums (2000 and 2300-engined cars) (all)

Dimensions (in/mm)

Wheelbase	101.5/2581mm (all)
Track	
Front	56.9/1445mm (all)
Rear	56/1422mm (all)
Overall length	170.9/4341mm (all)
Overall width	67/1703mm (all)
Overall height	53.7/1364mm (all)
Unladen weight	From 2205lb/1000kg (all)

More in this series:

This book describes the birth, development and rallying career of the Lancia Stratos, Europe's very first purpose-built rally car, in the mid/late 1970s, providing a compact and authoritative history of where, when and how it became so important to the sport. Also tells the story of the team.

ISBN: 978-1-787111-08-0
Paperback • 19.5x21cm
• 128 pages
• 131 colour and b&w pictures

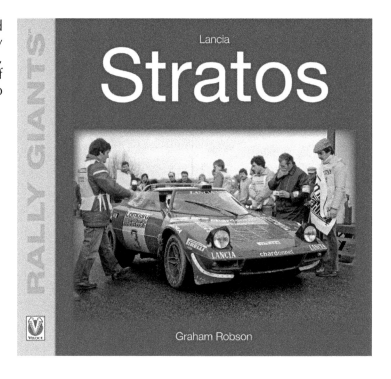

The Audi Quattro was the world's first successful four-wheel-drive rally car. It brought new standards to the sport, and inspired many others to copy it. This is the complete story.

ISBN: 978-1-787111-10-3
Paperback • 19.5x21cm
• 128 pages
• 116 colour and b&w pictures

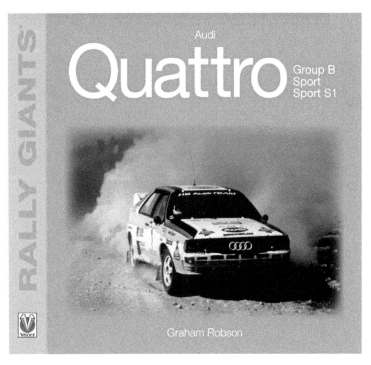

For more information and price details see **www.veloce.co.uk**
• email: info@veloce.co.uk • Tel: +44(0)1305 260068

The Escort MkI delivered everything its predecessor, the Lotus-Cortina, had promised. Versatile, accessible and competitive at all levels, it dominated international rallying throughout the 1970s, and became hugely popular with teams and spectators alike.

ISBN: 978-1-787111-07-3
Paperback • 19.5x21cm
• 128 pages
• 107 colour and b&w pictures

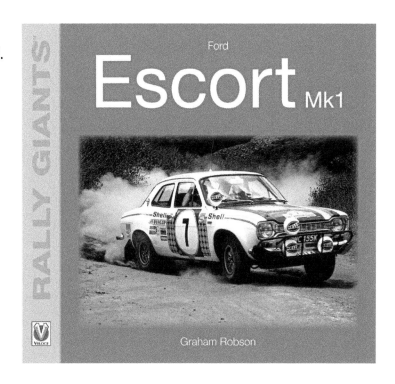

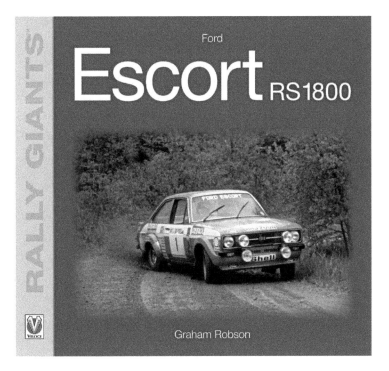

The Ford Escort MkII was a worthy successor to the original MkI. It became Ford's most successful rally car and the cars are still winning historic events today. It brought new standards to the sport, inspiring many others to copy it. Contains full details of every 'works' Escort MkII that went rallying, plus driver and personality profiles, and detailed car evolution.

ISBN: 978-1-787111-09-7
Paperback • 19.5x21cm • 128 pages • 112 colour and b&w pictures

For more information and price details see **www.veloce.co.uk**
• email: info@veloce.co.uk • Tel: +44(0)1305 260068

CORTINA

INDEX

20, 25, 29, 47

Panton, Howard 39
Pierpoint, Roy 75
Platt, Alan 48, 65
Porsche 64, 76

RAC 70
RAC Competitions Department/RAC MSA
  10, 52
Race Proved Savage 42-43, 113-14
Racing events:
  BRSCC/RAC British Saloon Car
    Championship 42, 51, 74-76
  European Saloon Car/Touring Car
    Championship 62, 74, 76-77, 80,
    121
  Austria 76
  Belgium/Spa 76, 85
  Brands Hatch 75-76
  Brands Hatch Six Hours 74, 77
  Goodwood 75
  France 80
  Marlborough 12 Hours 74
  Oulton Park Gold Cup 75
  Silverstone 77
  Switzerland 76, 80
  Zandvoort 74
Rallying events:
  Acropolis 63, 68, 71, 78
  (French) Alpine 63-68, 70-71, 85
  Circuit of Ireland 66
  East African Safari 62-63, 66-67,
    71, 73, 82-83
  Gulf London 66-67, 71, 78-79
  Jant 78

Liège (Spa)-Sofia-Liège 65-66, 68
London-Sydney Marathon 67, 71, 73
Midnight Sun 64
Monte Carlo 42, 63, 65, 70
Peking-Paris 1997 139
RAC 59, 63, 65-68, 70-71, 123
San Remo 70
Scottish 66-67, 69, 71, 87
Shell 4000 67, 71
Swedish 59, 67, 71-72
Three Cities 71
Tour de France 68
Tulip 63, 71
Welsh 70
World Cup (Daily Mirror) 42
[See also table 78-79]
Raviolo, Victor 13, 16
'Red Book' 10
Rees, Stan 21
Renault 7
Rental car fleets 105
Roberts, Dennis 15-16
Rolls-Royce (and Merlin engines) 7-8, 10,
  130
Roser, Len 110
Rugman, Malcolm 137
Ryan, Adrian 110

Saab 65
Sansom, Derek 136-137
Sanville, Steve 52
Sapino, Filippo 125
Sayle, Alexei 19, 132
Silverstone race circuit 25
Simister, Phil 29, 64
Snetterton racing circuit 54, 58
Standard-Triumph 9

Steele, Chris, Engineering 45
Superspeed 45, 114

Taurus 45
Taylor, Henry 48, 63-68, 70, 74, 76
Teesdale, Ken 20
Terrier sportscar 54
Terry, Len 54
Tomorrow's World 103
Toy, Sam 42, 95, 105, 111, 116, 120,
  123, 126, 131, 133-134
Trafalgar House Investments 131
Triumph 32, 65, 103
Trotman, Alex 12
Tustin, Martin 9
TVR 38

Uren, Jeff 42-43, 45, 114

Vauxhall 18, 26, 100-101, 134
Vignale 125
Villiers 51
Volkswagen 18
Volvo 63

Walker, Ian 45
Ward, Don 15
William Mills of Wednesbury 51
Willment 42, 45, 114
Willment, John 42, 73-75
Worters, Alan 17-18
Wyer, John 42

Young, John 14